P9-DKF-534

MODERN ECONOMIC ISSUES

OTTO ECKSTEIN, Harvard University, General Editor

In this series the great public issues in economics are posed and put in perspective by original commentary and reprints of the most interesting and significant recent statements by experts in economics and government.

BURTON A. WEISBROD, the editor of this volume, is currently Associate Professor of Economics at The University of Wisconsin. A former Senior Staff Member on the Presidents Council of Economic Advisers, he helped develop the Kennedy-Johnson Administrators' analysis which underlies the "Economic Opportunity Act" and the "War on Poverty." He is the author of *Economics of Public Health* and *External Benefits of Public Education*.

THE ECONOMICS OF POVERTY

AN AMERICAN PARADOX

Edited by Burton A. Weisbrod

PRENTICE-HALL, Inc., Englewood Cliffs, N.J.

Current printing (last number):
10 9 8 7 6 5 4 3 2

To Shirley, Linda, and Glen

PREFACE

This book focuses upon two questions concerning poverty which are of overriding importance:

1. Why does poverty exist today in the United States?
2. What can be done to minimize or eliminate poverty without impinging on other social and economic goals?

Regretfully, the answers are not apparent. The Introduction to this volume provides background information and perspective to help the reader analyze and find answers to the questions. The articles that follow present the diverse and frequently-conflicting points of view of a number of writers, both within and outside government, as to who the poor are and what can be done to help them. Somewhat surprising amidst this diversity is the thread of agreement that poverty is, indeed, not only a major problem, but one which demands federal government initiative to solve. *How major* the problem is, and *what kind* of government initiative—these are the issues that divide men.

In the course of writing my Introduction and selecting the papers to be included, I received very helpful suggestions from Professor Otto Eckstein and my colleagues at the University of Wisconsin, Professors Martin David, Harold Groves, and, especially, W. Lee Hansen and Robert J. Lampman. I wish to thank them and also Mr. Emmett Fenlon, who assisted me materially in countless ways.

B.A.W.

CONTENTS

ix

THE ECONOMICS OF POVERTY
An American Paradox

INTRODUCTION
THE ECONOMICS OF POVERTY:
AN AMERICAN PARADOX

Burton A. Weisbrod

WHAT IS POVERTY?

Poverty is as old as man. It is still the lot of most of the inhabitants of Asia, Africa, and Latin America. What, then, is new or different about poverty in the United States in the 1960s? The answer lies in the difference between *majority* poverty and *minority* poverty—between a poor nation and a wealthy nation. In a poor nation, the problem is to speed economic development—to expand *total* production. In the present-day United States, on the other hand, the economic system produces an annual income of some $7500 for the average family. Total output in the economy is adequate, right now, to provide reasonable living standards for all members of the society. The issue here is not whether poverty *can* be erased, but whether it *should* be, *how* and at *what speed!*

Although additional economic growth would reduce the frequency of poverty, as it has in the past, the United States already possesses the productivity to make a major cut in the numbers of poor people. This does not imply, however, that the devotion of more of the nation's resources to new and specific antipoverty measures will necessarily be more effective in reducing poverty than will their devotion to the expansion of existing programs, the enhancement of economic growth, or the elimination of racial discrimination. Neither does it imply anything about the effectiveness of the many specific antipoverty measures that have been proposed or are already in existence: the Johnson Administration's Economic Opportunity Act—with its Job Corps training program, community-action programs, and other provisions—(Article 9), education and manpower retraining, health and health insurance, public housing, urban renewal and regional development (as in Appalachia), Social Security, public assistance, minimum-wage increases and extensions, or negative income taxes, to name some of those discussed in the articles that follow.

It is paradoxical that, as the economy expanded and our ability to cope with poverty soared in the decades following World War II, general recognition of poverty's existence simultaneously waned. The explanation may lie in the "hidden" nature of poverty. It is true that the exodus to Suburbia and the increase in travel by superhighway and air rather than by city street and train have made it easier to ignore the tenements and shacks of urban slums and rural wastelands, to isolate the poor from the more fortunate majority. But part of the explanation lies in the gradual but continual diminution of poverty. The percentage of families with "low" incomes (less than $3000 in terms of 1962 purchasing power) dropped from 32 per cent in 1947 to 18 per cent in 1964. Even the absolute number of low-income families declined during this period, from 11 million to less than 9 million—and this happened at the same time that the total number of families in the United States grew from 37 million to 48 million.

If the poor are becoming less visible as well as less numerous, why is public attention to poverty increasing? Why was there less apparent concern about poverty ten or twenty years ago, when the poor were both more conspicuous and more numerous? There are no easy answers. But an analysis of the reasons for today's attention to poverty may help us to understand why that attention has grown.

The current interest in poverty has multiple roots. One is a growing concern about the unequal opportunities in the competition for income in our market economy. Another is concern about the outcome of that competition—that is, about the resulting income distribution. In other words, as some people see it, the problem is inequality—in education, in training, in employment; to others, the problem is the continuance of living standards which are so low as to seem abhorrent whatever the cause.

These two somewhat distinct bases for action help explain why a debate occurred within the federal administration during the fall and winter of 1963-64 on whether the goal of the emerging program was to increase opportunity or to decrease poverty. They also help explain the curious but little-noted contrast between what President Johnson calls the War on Poverty (*not* the War on Inequality of Opportunity) and the initial piece of supporting legislation, which is called the Economic Opportunity Act (*not* the Antipoverty Act)!

The desire to eliminate extremely low living standards or discriminatory barriers to equal opportunity, or both, provides two bases for action, but there are others as well. Many people wish to aid the *casualties* of economic progress—those workers for whom the growth and technological advance of the economy as a whole have meant a decreasing demand for their particular services and, hence, diminishing employment opportunities and earnings. This problem is illustrated by the depressed state of the Appalachian region, a depression largely traceable to the mechanization of coal-mining procedures and the growing competition offered by other fuels.

Still another basis of support for antipoverty measures stems from the desire of the more fortunate to escape the burdens that poverty imposes on them. Some of these costs of poverty to others involve transfer payments, such as the nearly $5 billion expended annually in public assistance. Others of these external diseconomies—such as occur through the fires, crimes and diseases slums breed—involve real losses to the society as a whole. The investment of resources to eliminate poverty would bring returns in the form of reductions in these social costs.

Thus, not all supporters of a more aggressive effort against poverty necessarily share the same motivation or the same objectives. But the noteworthy fact remains that the American people, acting through the federal government, have undertaken a major commitment to eliminate poverty in America. The Economic Opportunity Program, for which nearly 900 million dollars was authorized in its first year (1964), received a nearly doubled authorization in its second year, with further increases clearly in sight. Additional billions of dollars are flowing to other facets of President Johnson's antipoverty effort—to assist in the economic development of Appalachia, to strengthen elementary and secondary education for disadvantaged children, to provide health insurance for the aged, to strengthen the Manpower Development and Training Act and the Area Redevolpment Act, and so on.

EVOLUTION OF THE ANTIPOVERTY PROGRAM

Against this background, the origin and development of current federal antipoverty programs is an intriguing story. Of course, antecedents of the present attention to poverty are not difficult to find. In addition to the host of programs begun in the depression of the 1930s, social welfare measures have been initiated and expanded under every succeeding Administration. In 1949 the Joint Economic Committee (JEC) of Congress published its study, "Low-Income Families and Economic Stability," and in 1959 it commissioned another study, "The Low-Income Population and Economic Growth," as part of its broad study, "Employment, Growth, and Price Levels."

The federal program that is now emerging can be traced back to June 1963, when the Council of Economic Advisers (CEA) began to look beyond the dominant economic problem of the previous three years: the need to step up economic expansion so as to reduce the persistently high unemployment and underproduction. Not that the problem had been solved. But with a tax cut of over $11 billion well on its way toward passage (the Revenue Act of 1964), Walter W. Heller, Chairman of the CEA, his council members and staff—including Robert Lampman, who had authored the JEC Study Paper a few years earlier—began to lay the factual and analytical foundation for a possible 1964 attack on poverty. President Kennedy had indicated his interest—an interest aroused, in part, by Michael Harrington's *The Other America* and, in part, by his own experiences (particularly in West Virginia), during the 1960 Presidential campaign. Heller discussed the CEA's progress with President Kennedy on November 19, 1963—three days before the assassination—and was urged to continue efforts to bring the relevant agencies of government into consensus on a program.

One day after he became President in late November 1963, Lyndon Johnson made an enthusiastic decision to proceed with a review of the problem and potential methods for dealing with it. Within two months President Johnson announced an "unconditional war on poverty in America" in his State of the Union Message, and in his *Economic Report of the President* he set forth the broad outlines of the forthcoming antipoverty campaign. At the same time, the January 1964 *Annual Report* of the Council of Economic Advisers furnished the analytic base of the Administration's program (Article 5).

The program then moved into the legislative phase. Principal responsibility for fashioning specific legislation rested with the newly organized President's Task Force on the War Against Poverty, directed by Sargent Shriver. This was the forerunner of the Office of Economic Opportunity (OEO), established in August 1964 by the Economic Opportunity Act.

In many respects the key provision of the legislation fashioned by the Shriver Task Force was the establishment of the new administrative organ, the OEO. The OEO was given responsibility for coordinating not only the activities authorized by the act—the Job Corps, the Neighborhood Youth Corps, the local Community-Action Programs, the Volunteers in Service to America (a domestic Peace Corps), and so on—but all federal antipoverty measures. Although the advantages of such an integrating mechanism were potentially substantial, there were bound to be problems, too. Many of the programs to be coordinated were, or would be, administered by other agencies: the Department of Agriculture; the Department of Labor; the Department of Health, Education, and Welfare; and local governmental and private groups. Because the OEO's task would not be an easy one, the desirability of establishing a new level of authority became a lively issue (Article 10).

As congressional debate on the bill began, the political battlelines were sharply drawn. The bill was taken up first by the Ad Hoc Subcommittee on Poverty, of Congressman Adam Clayton Powell's (D., N.Y.) House Committee on Education and Labor Committee, and it was reported out on a straight party-line vote. When Congressman Peter Frelinghuysen (R., N.J.), ranking Republican member of that committee, testified later at the Senate hearings on the bill, he complained bitterly that Republican views had been disregarded, and that "Our committee was subjected to and yielded to intense political pressure." And he added, "You couldn't have a less bipartisan approach than we have had."

Division along party lines was less complete, although still apparent, in votes on the bill by the full Senate and House of Representatives. The political disagreement, however, centered on the best *means* by which to fight poverty. Frelinghuysen agreed that there was need "to prick the conscience of the nation that we have not done enough about poverty." Both the Republican Minority Statement and the Democratic Majority Statement in the JEC Report (Article 7) urged action. At no time, however, was the issue faced squarely as to whether poverty or unequal opportunity was the primary target of the program.

No one seemed to be arguing for any retrenchment of existing programs which either benefited the poor directly (Aid to Dependent Children, for example) or benefited a wider group that included the poor (for example, education, unemployment compensation, and Social Security). Rather, the disputes dealt with optimal methods of expanding efforts to eliminate poverty and equalize opportunity—in particular, whether conventional approaches should be strengthened or new ones adopted. Thus, if there was an ingredient of politics in the antipoverty recipe, there was, and is, also a sizable and dominant element of humanitarianism.

POVERTY AND THE ECONOMIC PROBLEM

Compassion for the poor is perhaps a helpful—but not a sufficient—foundation upon which to build an effective antipoverty program. Although there is consensus that poverty exists in America today, there remain honest and serious disagreements about its causes, scope, magnitude, and remedies. But the wisdom of devoting a given amount of money to an antipoverty program, and the most effective way to spend that money, ought to depend not merely on *whether* a problem exists, but also on *how many* poor people there are, *why* they are poor, and *where* they are located.

Even if satisfactory answers to these questions could be obtained—
and complete answers are too much to hope for—another important but
deeply troubling question would remain: How should the problem be
attacked? How can the vicious cycle in which poverty is transmitted from
generation to generation be broken? Can the present generation of adult
poor be helped materially by health, education, and retraining programs,
for example, or is their only hope to receive transfer payments from the
more fortunate members of society? What is the appropriate balance
between investment expenditures designed to increase the future productivity of the current poor, and transfer payments to provide immediate
assistance?

Answers to these and related questions involve choice—which is the
essence of any economic problem. In the pages that follow, a number of
choices will be presented—on the basis of which public policy will
ultimately rest. But if choice is at the base of economic problems, balancing at the margin is at the base of solutions. When there are two or
more means of achieving some end, economic analysis is likely to conclude that the selection should neither be one nor the other, but some
combination of the various alternatives. So it is with the campaign
against poverty.

One criterion by which to judge programs is their relative effectiveness. But another related criterion concerns the effect of the program
on the consumers' freedom to decide how to spend their income. Thus,
Milton Friedman (Article 15) and Irving Kristol (Article 13) argue for
cash transfers (rather than aid in the form of free or subsidized goods
and services) on the ground that the poor can—and ought to—decide
how to handle their own poverty problems. By contrast, the CEA and the
OEO are predisposed to avoid increasing transfer payments whenever
possible. They favor an expansion of government investment expenditures designed to raise the productivity and future income of the poor—
particularly of today's children and youth. Thus, another choice is implicit in these alternative routes: How much public funds should be
devoted to alleviating the poverty of today's adults and preventing future poverty of today's children, respectively? No one is indifferent to
the desirability of doing both, but the limitations of the public purse
make it necessary to choose between the two emphases.

As alternatives are considered, the advantages of particular antipoverty
measures should be examined in the light of the availability of resources
they will require. If a prospective program requires resources that are
already in short supply—trained social workers, for example—then the
wisdom of adopting the program may be questionable. Initiation of the

new program would bring a contraction of other programs presently assisting the needy. Such scarcity of supply is, of course, a short-run problem, for in time more skilled personnel can be trained. But in the interim, resource availability should be reckoned with in the development of an effective program. Here is yet another choice: whether to devote resources to expanding the supply of skilled personnel or to substitute other programs that are less likely to encounter resource bottlenecks.

THERE IS POVERTY IN THE UNITED STATES, BUT HOW MUCH?

The CEA counts 35 million poor people in the United States. Michael Harrington accepts Leon Keyserling's estimate of 40-50 million. Herman Miller, of the U.S. Bureau of the Census, has stated that more than 23 million people are poor enough to qualify for public assistance in their own states. One might ask: What difference does it make whether there are 23 million or 50 million poor? As Galbraith puts it, no precise measure—no precise definition—of poverty is needed ". . . save as a tactic for countering the intellectual obstructionist. . . ."

Is it that simple? Is it obstructionist to argue that the proper course of action is not clear until we know how large the job is? Until we know more about why the poor are poor, where the poor are located, what really constitutes poverty?

Yes and no. Choice, once again, is involved. As is true of most problems, the information available is less than complete while the objectives are complex and not fully understood. And so society must weigh the advantages of delay—which would provide time to learn more about poverty and how best to attack it—against the advantages of speedy action. More information can be obtained, but only by further delaying the fight against poverty. Thus there is a case for prompt action, for going ahead without more information and more precise measures of poverty.

But there is also a case for caution. A careful, well-specified, definition of poverty is not an academic frill, something that policy-makers can dispense with. Without an operational definition of poverty to make clear who is eligible for help, it is unlikely that any antipoverty effort will be effective. Without a careful definition of poverty to guide public officials, funds allocated to strengthen the education of the poor will become support for education of all children. However desirable such support may be, it will do little to help the neediest. Without an operational definition of poverty, the Economic Opportunity Act's Community-Action Program

—intended to stimulate local leadership in an attack against the special poverty problems it confronts—will become a political pork-barrel measure in which funds are thinned out so as to provide federal money for every Congressman's district. Lacking a careful definition of poverty, we will be unable to assess the effectiveness of proposed efforts to curb it. We cannot tell whether or not we are succeeding unless we have a way of measuring achievement. And if we are to have a gauge, we must have an operational definition of what we are trying to eliminate: poverty.

What, then, is the appropriate balance between speedy action and the collection of additional information about the nature and magnitude of the problem? Much depends on our sense of urgency, our confidence in the efficacy of the proposed solutions, and our willingness to make decisions which may turn out to have been incorrect. It is always possible to postpone action until more has been learned about the nature of a problem and its possible solutions. Postponement reduces the likelihood of adopting measures that might later prove unsuccessful. But it also increases the likelihood of delaying the adoption of programs that might be effective. It is unfortunate, but true, that the probability of making an error of commission can be reduced, but only by increasing the probability of making an error of omission. At the same time it is true that with poverty as, indeed, with all other problems, inaction is itself a decision. There is no way out of the dilemma. A decision—a choice—cannot be avoided.

HOW SHOULD POVERTY BE DEFINED AND MEASURED?

At a broad, conceptual level most people would agree that *poverty* means *an inadequate level of consumption.* That is, poverty is a matter of having insufficient food, clothing, or shelter. But what is meant by an "inadequate" level of consumption? How should the level of consumption be measured? Is a family that lives in a dilapidated shack without indoor plumbing necessarily poor—even if it has a television set and a car? The Minority Republican statement about the War on Poverty (Article 7) raises some provocative questions along these lines.

There have been investigations—particularly by the Department of Agriculture, the Bureau of Labor Statistics, and the Social Security Administration—to determine the needs of families of various types, sizes, ages, and locations. Standards of dietary adequacy have been established. Objective standards for clothing and housing needs, however, are more elusive, for these involve the services of durable goods—services which are yielded over time. Consequently, "adequacy" of living conditions is determined by the stock of clothing and housing the consumer owns, as well as by the flow of nondurable food items he buys during a given period.

The difficulties of establishing standards of adequate consumption levels are matched by the difficulties of measuring the actual consumption levels of particular families and individuals. Thus, income has come to be generally accepted as a useful measure of living standard, the implicit assumption being that current income is a reasonably good indicator of current consumption levels. There has been, of course, considerable disagreement over the appropriate level of income to use. Writing only a few years apart, Galbraith (Article 3), Keyserling (Article 14), and the CEA (Article 5) used family incomes of $1000, $4000, and $3000, respectively, as measures of poverty.

The $3000 Poverty Line

The $3000 figure, although originally adopted by the Johnson Administration as a rough measure of poverty, was acknowledged to be unsatisfactory for determining eligibility for specific antipoverty programs. It was generally agreed that no single measure based on current money income alone could be applied satisfactorily to families of all sizes and in all circumstances.

One of the objections to the $3000 line was that it overstated the number of "truly" poor families by including small, two-person families with money incomes up to $3000. It turned out, however, that if a variable poverty line were used (centering on $3000 for a family of four but adding or subtracting, as necessary, $500 per person for larger and smaller families), the number of poor people would actually increase by more than a million. The increase consisted of children; the number of adults dropped.

Criticism of the $3000 poverty line was not limited to its failure to take into account the size of the family. It was also attacked for relying on money income alone as a measure of poverty. After all, argued the critics, does not this measure disregard the real, but nonmoney, income received by people who live in their own homes and therefore do not have to pay rent? Does it not disregard entirely the value of food produced in gardens and on family farms—food which substitutes for money income? Moreover, they pointed out, the federal government actually publishes data that include not only cash incomes, but also the estimated value of income from owner-occupied housing, food produced and consumed on family farms, and some other types of nonmoney income, and these figures show markedly less "poverty."

It was true. The Department of Commerce has provided annual estimates not only for the distribution of money income, but also of personal income—that is, money income plus "imputed" income in the nonmoney forms mentioned above. However, the personal-income data are based upon federal income tax returns; these are not a good source of information because in some cases incomes may be so low as to make unnecessary the filing of income tax returns. Moreover, not much is known about the amount of *non*money incomes received by families with low levels of money income.

The data used by the CEA refer to money income only, and they were obtained from direct household surveys. At the same time, money-income data may be misleading because the tendency of most people is to understate their incomes (although most of the underreporting seems to occur at higher income levels). The issues of underreporting, income-in-kind, and statistical accuracy are not quantitatively trivial, for their effect is to reduce the number of low-income families from the 9 million which are reported to have money incomes below $3000 to the 6 million which have personal incomes below $3000. Concern about the adequacy of the personal-income series, however, led the Commerce Department in 1965 to suspend publishing it until new source materials and improved estimating techniques could be applied. As the series is reconstructed, one of the major aims will be to relate it to the existing series on cash incomes.

Although the effect of adjusting for underreporting and income-in-kind is to cut the number of poor, other factors—such as extraordinary medical care needs and the dearth of public services available to rural and farm families—tend to raise the number who would be regarded as poor by a more comprehensive measure. (There are also regional cost-of-living differences to consider, but their effect on the total number of poor, although difficult to judge, is probably quite small.)

A more fundamental question involves the meaning of the $3000 figure. Is it intended to mean (or, in any case, should it mean): (a) that at least $3000 in total command over goods and services is required for nonpoverty living, or (b) that at least $3000 of money income and some "normal" amounts of nonmoney income and of assets are required? If concept (a) is appropriate, then money-income figures alone clearly understate the number of families that can consume at least $3000 of goods and services in a year, and thereby they overstate the amount of poverty —as the critics have argued—for some people with inadequate current money incomes have supplementary nonmoney income or assets to fall back upon. But if concept (b) is appropriate, then many of the attacks on the data are unwarranted. In fact, the number of poor may be even greater than the 35 million estimated, for some families with money incomes not far above $3000 may have so few assets and so little income-in-kind that they might be properly regarded as poor.

Some New Measures of Poverty

A recent study by Mollie Orshansky of the Social Security Administration (SSA)[1] presented a new and more complex measure of poverty—one which consists of a separate variable poverty line for farm and for nonfarm families of various sizes and age composition, adjusted for nonmoney incomes. Based on Department of Agriculture estimates of food requirements, this study proposes a poverty line ranging from $1540 for a single person and $3130 for a nonfarm family of four to $5090 for a family of seven or more. It reduces these amounts by 40 per cent for farm families to account for the value of food produced and consumed on the farm, and to account for the greater frequency of home ownership (and, hence, of imputed rental income) among such families.[2] This approach—which was adopted by the OEO in May 1965—indicates approximately the same total number of poor persons (around 34 million) as does the flat $3000-per-family and $1500-per-individual standard used previously by the CEA.

The characteristics of the poor, however, are considerably different if the SSA standards are used. The number of farm residents classified as poor falls by over one third, from 4.9 million to 3.2 million. The number of children rises by 40 per cent, from 10.8 million to 15 million. The number of aged poor families drops precipitously, from 3.1 million to 1.5 million. Thus, the more sophisticated approach shifts emphasis away from the aged and farmers, and toward large families and children.

Whichever concept is adopted, it is clear that low income in any single year does not necessarily constitute poverty. This is particularly true if accumulated net assets (i.e., assets minus debts) are available to tide a family over its temporary drop in income, or if the family is able to borrow on the strength of its potential future income. Assets owned by low-income families are, as expected, generally small. According to a recent study by the Federal Reserve Board, half of all families with incomes under $3000 owned assets of $2760 or less. Some low-income persons owned great wealth, however, as indicated by the fact that average (mean) asset holdings were three times that size. The combination of small incomes and large holdings of assets is not common, but it is most likely to be found among elderly, retired persons. Nevertheless, most of the elderly who are poor in terms of income are also short of assets. The use of accumulated assets (and borrowing) to maintain consumption levels when income is temporarily or chronically depressed is reflected in data on consumer expenditure patterns. Data gathered by the Bureau of Labor Statistics for use in reweighting the consumer price index indicated that families with annual money incomes under $3000 actually spent more than $120 on consumption for every $100 of income.

If a drop in income in any given year does not necessarily mean poverty, then neither does a rise in income in any given year mean that poverty has been left behind. A long-standing deficiency of consumer durable goods (such as home furnishings) and inadequate housing may not be offset by a temporary rise in income. Neither can many nutritional defects be overcome by a temporary improvement in diet.

The January 1965 *Report* of the CEA (Article 6) provides new and revealing information about the temporary nature of low income among various population groups. Among families that were classified as poor in 1962—that is, that had money incomes under $3000—69 per cent were also poor in 1963; of the remainder, two fifths moved above the $3000 mark—but not far: they still had incomes under $4000. Thus it cannot be said that most poverty is only temporary. Much more must be learned about the income patterns of particular families over long periods, if not over the family life cycle.

On the other hand, if poverty persisted into the second year for 70-80 per cent of the families, then for 20-30 per cent it did not. If this process continues, so that each year as few as 20 per cent escaped poverty— and if that percentage were distributed randomly among the poor—then after, say five years, only 80% × 80% × 80% × 80% × 80%, or 33 per cent of the original group would be left. The other 67 per cent would have escaped poverty—although not necessarily permanently. This is rather optimistic, however, because those leaving poverty are not likely to be randomly selected. Furthermore, some whose incomes rise above the poverty line may fall back below it within a short time. Additional data on the "turnover rate" among the poor—or, what is equivalent, the duration of low income status—is sorely needed.

As we sum up this brief survey of the issues involved in deciding how widespread poverty is, it must be said that the critics of the war on poverty—whether they disagree with specific measures or with the effort as a whole—are right in one respect: it does make a difference how *poverty* is defined. The number of the poor differs according to the definition used. Yet the proponents of prompt action are also right: whichever definition is used, there is much poverty to be found.

More important, perhaps, than the total number of poor is the composition of the group. This characteristic is quite sensitive to the measure of poverty that is used. A measure that adjusts for family size and that accounts for assets and nonmoney income will tend to exclude many of the aged families, and particularly those living on farms; it will increase the absolute and relative number of children who are classified in poor families, and will increase the absolute and relative number of Negroes classified as poor. The poor families will be, predominantly, the younger and larger families, and children will constitute a larger fraction of the total group. On the other hand, any measure of poverty that includes medical needs and income prospects (particularly as the latter influence the ability to borrow) will cause many of the aged to be classified as poor. Thus effective allocation of a limited antipoverty budget will vary —perhaps drastically—with the poverty measure that is applied.

IS POVERTY A RELATIVE MATTER?

Standards of poverty vary from nation to nation, from region to region, and from time to time. In the late 1940s, a $2000 annual family-income figure was used to measure poverty in the United States; by 1957, the figure of $2500 was common; and today the figure is $3000. Much of this increase reflects adjustments for rising prices. Yet if the $2000 income poverty line of 1947 had been held constant, except for increases in consumer prices, today it would amount to $2750 (not $3000) and the number of families considered poor would be smaller by more than 800,000. The fact is that our notion of what constitutes a satisfactory standard of living has changed.

To some people, the raising of the poverty line seems improper; to others it is desirable and even necessary that standards of poverty should rise, reflecting the society's general economic progress. Thus it has been proposed by Victor Fuchs, of the National Bureau of Economic Research, that all families with incomes less than one half the national median family income should be considered poor. This approach would produce a poverty line rising over time, and it would make the prevalence of poverty depend on the distribution of income as well as on its absolute level. Startlingly, this measure shows that no progress has been made against poverty in the United States between 1947 and 1962: approximately 20 per cent of all families have been classed as poor throughout the period. In short, despite a general rise in income, its distribution has changed little.

It is obvious that the difficulty of reducing the number and percentage of poor families will be greater if the standards imposed are relative and, hence, rise over time. If the standard of poverty is constantly rising, is the war against poverty not hopeless? It is probably true that poverty can never be ended once and for all. With good luck, a buoyant economy, and imaginative programs, we may be able to erase poverty—as it is currently defined—within our lifetime. But before that time the definition of what constitutes a substandard level of living, poverty, or need may have changed. Thus the struggle against poverty is a continuing one. Nevertheless, even if society's concept of poverty were certain to change, it would not follow that we should be any less concerned about those who are poor by present standards.

WHO ARE THE POOR, AND WHY ARE THEY POOR?

The poor can be described in countless ways. To be useful, descriptions of poverty should relate to its causes in particular cases. Such descriptions may suggest policies for the prevention and elimination of poverty. The article by Harry G. Johnson proposes, in effect, to describe the poor as (1) those for whom the economy has failed to provide jobs, (2) those whose ability to contribute to the productive process is insufficient, and (3) those whose opportunities to participate in the productive process are restricted by discrimination of various kinds. It may not be easy to fit the poor neatly into one or another category. Without an analytic framework, however, descriptions of the poor in terms of demographic and social characteristics—such as age, color and sex—tend to obscure the fact that the same antipoverty remedies may apply to people with different characteristics.

The Importance of Employment Opportunities

One useful dimension by which to describe the poor is the *employment status* of the family breadwinner. Are families poor because the breadwinner is chronically unemployed? If so, a more rapidly expanding economy with increasing employment opportunities will contribute substantially to the elimination of poverty. In 1963 there were 9 million families with money incomes under $3000; the heads of 1.4 million of these families worked only at part-time jobs while the heads of another 1.8

million families worked at full-time jobs but for less than fifty weeks out of the year. For these 3.2 million families (2.6 million out of 7.2 million if the variable poverty line of the ssa is used), full employment and economic growth could mean substantial alleviation of their poverty. These families, however, comprise only about one third of the poor.

Some of the impact of economic expansion on employment opportunities can be observed in data on the changing distribution of families according to their number of wage earners. During 1963, a year of rapid economic expansion, the number of families in the United States with no wage earners decreased by 300,000; meanwhile, the number of families with two wage earners increased by 300,000, and the number with three or more wage earners increased by 500,000. This contributed to a reduction of 300,000 in the number of poor families (covering a million or more individuals).

This information points to the opportunities for poor people to shift from one descriptive category to another. These shifts among groups may be even more significant than increases of income within groups. It is clear that economic expansion tends to shift men from the "unemployed" to the "employed" category. But that expansion may cut poverty among families headed by females, or among migrant labor families (to cite but two examples), is usually—and erroneously—denied. In an economy with high unemployment, poverty-stricken fathers may leave their families in order that the children might become eligible for relief benefits. In an expanding economy, fewer such broken families are likely to be created in the first place, and those that exist are more likely to escape from poverty as reunification of the family or remarriage brings a breadwinner and transfers the unit out of the class of "female-head" families. Similarly, although economic expansion may not raise incomes in the migrant labor group, it may help provide opportunities for members of that group to find more remunerative industrial employment.

Whatever the effect of economic expansion on particular groups of low-income families and individuals, its effect on the total amount of poverty is powerful. One way of seeing this is to divide the fifteen years 1948-63 into categories of strong economic expansion (1950, 1951, 1953, 1955, 1959, and 1962), slow expansion (1952, 1956, 1960, and 1963), and no expansion (1949, 1954, 1957, 1958, and 1961), and then to note what happened to the amount of poverty during each group of years. If the $3000 family-income measure is used, the results show that in years of strong expansion, the number of poor families declined by an average of 667,000 per year; in the slow-expansion years the decline was a third less: 425,000 families per year; and in the no-expansion years of downturn or recession, the number of poor families *rose* by 400,000 per year. Thus, the difference between strong expansion and recession has been more than a million families (from a decrease of 667,000 to an increase of 400,000) among the poor. Similar effects are seen in the number of cases requiring general assistance: in the years of greatest expansion welfare rolls were cut by an average of 63,000 cases annually, but they were reduced by an average of only 5000 in the slow-expansion years, and were *increased* by 71,000 in the years of recession.

The primary connection between economic expansion and poverty is employment opportunity. Economic expansion and technological change bring their own adjustment problems, however, for some workers are displaced by capital equipment. Even when the total demand for labor is increased, changes in its composition may eliminate employment opportunities or reduce income for particular workers, sometimes adding them to the rolls of the unemployed and the poor. Large concentrations of poverty are found among workers attached to such declining industries as agriculture and coal mining. Gunnar Myrdal (Article 18) argues that this technological or "structural" unemployment is an important cause of poverty. He urges adoption of an active labor-market policy, as Sweden has, to match workers and employment opportunities through retraining and relocation programs and similar measures.

Inability to Contribute Substantially to Output

As we try to understand why poverty exists in the United States and how it is related to economic change and growth, we must recognize that some people are unable to take advantage of the opportunities growth provides. One reason for this inability may be *poor health*. The U.S. National Health Survey has found that persons in low-income families **are** absent from work or badly disabled for more days during the year —and, in the case of children, lose more time from school because of illness—than do persons in higher-income families. The 15 million children of low-income families visit physicians only half as often as other children do. A majority of those between the ages of five and fourteen have never been to a dentist; and although they enter the hospital less often, they stay twice as long as do children from higher-income families.

Inability to benefit from economic growth may also be the result of *age*. (The aged comprise between one fifth and one third of the poor, depending on whether the ssa measure or the $3000 measure of poverty is used.) The prominence of the nonworking aged among the poor reinforces the view that a significant part of the poverty problem is immune to short-run increases in economic opportunities. Further analysis of the age characteristics of the poor indicates that nearly 10 per cent (by either measure) are headed by young people in the fourteen-to-twenty-four-year bracket. For many of them low income is a temporary situation, a consequence of job inexperience that will be rectified in time.

Relative inability to benefit from economic growth may result from *family responsibility.* In our society, a broken family—that is, one headed by a female—is very likely to find itself in severe financial straits. A mother with young children is expected to care for them, not to be in the labor market. Even if the mother attempts to enter the labor market, she is handicapped by the need to pay someone else to care for her children. Thus, it is not surprising to learn that more than 40 per cent (by either measure) of all families headed by a female were in poverty status in 1963.

An inability to take advantage of expanding opportunities may also arise from *inadequate training and education.* There is weighty evidence to indicate that education is at the core of any successful campaign against poverty. Among families[3] with income under $3000 in 1961, 61 per cent were headed by persons who had no more than an elementary education. By contrast, only 7 per cent of the poor families were headed by persons who had obtained some college education. Among families headed by a person with eight years of schooling or less, more than one out of three were poor. This was more than three times the proportion of families headed by a high school graduate who were poor, and nearly five times the proportion of families headed by a person with some college education who were poor.

The relationship between education, productivity, and earning capacity is so powerful that it transcends some of the discriminatory income barriers that confront nonwhites. A nonwhite family headed by a person with some college education is less than one third as likely to be poor as a similar nonwhite family headed by a person who has gone no further than elementary school.

Lack of education, together with poor health and disability, is a major contributor to low productivity and low income. It is startling to realize that 2 million families are poor (by either the $3000 measure or the SSA measure), even though headed by a person who worked at a full-time job throughout the entire year of 1963 (fifty weeks or more). The productivity of these workers was so low that they could not earn even the $1.50 per hour that would bring a full-time worker $3000 of annual income. (An increase of the federal minimum wage to the $1.50 level is advocated as an antipoverty measure by Leon Keyserling [Article 14], but Milton Friedman [Article 15] argues that this would increase, rather than decrease, poverty.)

Discrimination

Any description of the poor which attempts to define causes of poverty must include color. A nonwhite family is more than two and a half times as likely to be poor as a white family. In 1963, 44 per cent of all nonwhite families were poor, compared with 16 per cent of all white families (by either the $3000 measure or the ssa measure). The median income of all nonwhite families is only $3465 per year, compared with $6548 for white families. As Alan Batchelder's article points out, these figures understate nonwhite poverty because they disregard—among other things—the effects of housing discrimination on the rents nonwhites must pay.

Much, but not all, of the excess poverty among nonwhites is directly attributable to educational deficiencies. At every level of schooling—as measured by years, not quality—the percentage of nonwhite families that is poor greatly exceeds the percentage of white families that is poor. For example, among white families headed by a high school graduate, 11 per cent are poor, while among nonwhites the figure is 30 per cent.

When a nonwhite family becomes poor, it is more likely to remain poor. The CEA 1965 *Report* shows that the rate at which particular families move out of poverty is markedly lower for nonwhites than it is for whites. Of the families classified as poor in 1962, 33 per cent of the white families—but only 24 per cent of the nonwhite families—had escaped in 1963. In short, low income is only temporary for relatively more white families than nonwhite families. Moreover, of those families whose incomes did rise from less than $3000 in 1962 to more in 1963, 58 per cent of the white families had sizable income increases—to $4000 or more —while only 43 per cent of the nonwhite families scored comparable increases. In terms of severity and tenacity, poverty among nonwhites is more serious than previous data seemed to imply.

Progress against poverty has been made by both whites and nonwhites, but to different extents. Between 1947 and 1963 the number of families that had incomes under $3000 fell by 45 per cent for whites, but only by 34 per cent for nonwhites. To some extent, however, the slower progress made by nonwhites is explained by their more rapid rate of population growth. This produced a relatively larger increase in the number of young, low-income families among nonwhites than among whites.

employment opportunities sufficiently to bring the unemployment rate down to the 4 per cent (or lower) level that is generally considered "full" employment. Aggregate economic policy—both fiscal and monetary—could be used to fight poverty still more aggressively. Moreover, stimulation of the economy is not necessarily an alternative to the more individualistic approach of worker retraining, aid to education, and other investments in human productivity. Both can well be used.

To what extent should a new and more vigorous attack on poverty consist of federally directed programs, state and local programs, or private measures?

The issue is not simply whether *any* federal action is required—although that, too, has been questioned—but whether such federal action as is taken should involve federal control. The federal government might, for example, grant funds to states for use against poverty as they see fit, or it might allow federal income-tax credits (not merely deductions) for private gifts to philanthropic organizations helping the poor.

Much of the congressional debate over the Economic Opportunity Act was basically concerned with the degree of centralization appropriate for the program. C. Lowell Harriss (Article 10), questioned the wisdom of vesting broad authority in the director of the OEO.* Republicans and Democrats expressed their traditionally divergent views regarding the advantages and disadvantages of centralized decision-making and the respective roles to be played by state and local governments and by private groups.

To what extent should resources in the war on poverty be devoted to seeking solutions to the short-run problem versus the long-run problem?

Certain means are ineffective in fighting poverty in the short run— that is, the poverty currently in existence. It is too late to prevent poverty among the already aged. With some exceptions, all that can be done for this group is to alleviate its poverty by programs transferring to it income from the more prosperous elements of the population. Prevention of poverty is also largely impossible for nonaged, but mature, adults. For this group, however, rehabilitation efforts—involving such measures as training, retraining, and relocation—are real possibilities for enhancing productivity and employability.

Hopes for combatting poverty in the long run are highest for young children, because effective action may prevent their becoming poor

---

* President Johnson has given the director of the OEO, Sargent Shriver, the additional task of coordinating all federal antipoverty activities, including those which fall beyond the scope of the Economic Opportunity Act. The director's coordinating role is, to a great degree, the distinctive provision of the Act, and the source of considerable disagreement between the political parties.

adults. Many heads of poor families today are poor because of "mistakes" made during their childhood and youth by their parents or society —particularly mistakes concerning the health, education, and training expenditures that could have been so influential in raising their future productivity and earning capacity. (The ability of a family to make these expenditures depends, in part, on the number of children it has; thus, large family size intensifies the financial problems that low income brings.)

It perhaps goes without saying that no prevention program can ever be completely successful: there will always be some adults who—because of mental or physical disabilities or because of declining demand for their skills—are earning low incomes in spite of society's best efforts. Thus, some resources will inevitably have to be devoted to the rehabilitation of the poor and the alleviation of poverty. The issue, however, is whether the balance now struck among the alternatives is optimal.

Discussions of "hard-core" poverty (see, for example, Articles 3 and 18 by Galbraith and Myrdal) implicitly consider the problem in short-run terms. Opportunities for dealing with poverty among today's illiterate adults are, indeed, limited; but it may be possible to prevent today's youth from becoming the illiterate adults of the future. Similarly, rapid economic growth will not help today's retired citizens markedly; but by reducing unemployment and increasing earnings and savings among members of the current labor force, it can lower the chances of their being poor after reaching retirement age.

To what extent should resources be devoted to helping a depressed region expand economically in order to assist its poor residents, rather than to helping its needy residents directly?

Specifically, should an antipoverty program be designed to help Appalachia or Appalachians? The fundamental approach of the Economic Opportunity Act of 1964 is to help the residents directly. It adopts the long-run preventive approach: most of its funds go for education, training, and local community programs, all of which are aimed principally at children and young people, wherever they live.

By contrast, the Appalachia Regional Development Act emphasizes the construction of roads and airport facilities, the development of hydro-electric power and other natural resources, and, in general, investment in the region rather than in its inhabitants. Of the $1.1 billion allocated to this program in 1965, $840 million is earmarked for roads and highways. Investment in the transportation and communications facilities and natural resources of the region will help to attract industry and commerce, thereby expanding employment opportunities and reducing poverty. In this way, mobility of capital is being counted upon to be the springboard from poverty for the residents of Appalachia.

Alternatively, the poor could be assisted to move from depressed areas to regions in which economic opportunities are expanding, or they could be provided with the information, education, and training to facilitate out-migration. In short, mobility of population or mobility of capital—or both—could be effective in the antipoverty struggle. But which combination is best? Are regional development programs—whether for Appalachia, the Upper Great Lakes region, or the Ozark plateau—and the Economic Opportunity Program parts of a consistent and effective antipoverty effort? The answers are not clear.

To what extent should general measures which benefit both the poor and nonpoor be adopted, and to what extent should measures be directed specifically at the poor?

The choice is not as simple as it seems. It is often very difficult to identify and reach the poor. Thus, more general measures may be more useful although seemingly less efficient. President Johnson regards the Appalachia Regional Program and Medicare as part of the War on Poverty, although two thirds of the residents of Appalachia and the majority of the aged covered by Social Security are not poor. And, as another part of its antipoverty effort, the Administration sponsored and the Congress enacted, a $1 billion program of federal aid to elementary and secondary schools for fiscal year 1966, even though one of two criteria for allocating funds among the states—namely, the existing level of educational expenditures per student in each state—gave more help to the wealthier states.

It is not really unusual for social welfare measures to have their principal impact on the nonpoor. The Social Security program of old-age, survivors', and disability insurance does not benefit some of the poor (particularly nonwhites, as Alan Batchelder notes in Article 8)—because they were not employed in jobs covered by the legislation. The same is true of unemployment insurance, which excludes millions of workers from coverage and does not extend to chronic unemployment. Similarly, as Sar Levitan points out (Article 16), the United States Employment Service uses screening and testing devices that are suitable for the majority of job applicants, but not for the uneducated and illiterate poor.

In all these cases, the elimination of poverty is only one of the goals of the program—and, with multiple goals, conflicts develop. The aid-to-education bill, for example, was considered by some federal legislators —particularly those from the South—to constitute support for impoverished areas, which are more common in the South than elsewhere in the country. To some legislators from the more prosperous industrial states of the North, however, the focus on poverty appeared to be a useful device for initiating a general program of federal aid to education. Even a staunch believer in antipoverty programs may understand—although he may not forgive—skeptics who wonder where the efforts are heading when measures whose primary impact is on the nonpoor are defended on antipoverty grounds.

To what extent should aid to the poor be provided without restrictions on the way it is used?

The alternative is not simply to provide assistance in cash rather than in the form of goods and services, because the use of cash could also be restricted. The problem is: Should poor people decide how their poverty problems are best dealt with, or should someone else decide—perhaps a federal, state, or local government official or board, or a community philanthropy? This brings into sharp focus the interrelatedness of "efficiency" considerations—the effectiveness of alternatives—and "equity" considerations—the fairness of these alternatives. It also makes clear how conflicts can develop in the pursuit of multiple goals. What should be done if taxpayers, who provide the help for the poor, prefer a course of action which the poor oppose?

Among the numerous solutions proposed in the articles below, some —such as those involving unrestricted cash grants and tax reductions or rebates to the poor—would provide maximum freedom of choice to the poor. Other programs, such as the Job Corps or the Neighborhood Youth Corps established by the Economic Opportunity Act, help the poor only if they participate in a particular program.

Nevertheless, even devices for transferring money to the poor without restrictions have an influence on their behavior. The possibility cannot be disregarded that such transfers might affect their motivation to work and earn or even to have additional children. These potential incentive effects form the basis for many of the objections to the proposal to end poverty by large-scale income transfers. Note that because the average family with money income under $3000 has only $1800, transfers of at least $1200 per family—or $11 billion for the 9 million low-income families—would be required (the sum would rise with increases in the effect of such transfers on incentives). Currently, little is known about this effect, and we can only guess at its significance. Of course, the work-disincentive effects for those of the poor who are aged or permanently disabled would be limited.

As these various issues and alternative or complementary courses of actions are considered, it is important to remember that society needs to look—and, indeed, does look—not only at the benefits of a particular program but also at its costs. *Cost* and *expenditures* may not be synonymous. When labor is unemployed and capital equipment underutilized, an increase in government or private expenditures might require no withdrawal of resources from other uses, and, hence, no real or social costs. The additional expenditures could attract previously idle resources into productive use. By contrast, sharp expansion of expenditures on specific programs such as education and retraining might require resources—notably trained teachers—which are already fully employed.

LEARNING HOW TO CUT POVERTY

Resources for an attack on poverty are not unlimited and, as a result, choices must be made—between centralized and decentralized programs; between provisions of goods or services and cash aid; between prevention, rehabilitation, and alleviation; between investment in people and investment in physical capital; between measures aimed specifically at the poor and more general programs; and so on. In no case must we select one alternative alone; a combination—a mixed strategy—may be preferable. Efficient selection among alternatives requires, however, an understanding of the effectiveness of each type of program, and knowledge about the degree to which each reinforces or conflicts with the others.

How can more be learned about effective ways to eliminate poverty? Somehow the questions raised earlier are being answered, if not explicitly through thought and discussion, then implicitly as courses of action are proposed and adopted. As antipoverty measures are initiated, are steps also being taken to insure that we learn from our experience? Will we know more three or four years from now than we do today about the effectiveness of various approaches? the most effective combination of programs? the speed with which each should be undertaken? Because poverty is produced by many forces, will it be possible to tell at some future date how much of the observed reduction in poverty can be attributed to each of the antipoverty programs, or even how much can be attributed to the combined effect of all of them? Do not forget that poverty in the United States declined dramatically between 1947 and 1964—from 32 per cent to 19 per cent of all families—even without any of the antipoverty programs now being introduced, although continual increases in social welfare expenditures did occur during this period.

Unless steps are taken in the early stages of a project's development to facilitate its later evaluation, serious misinterpretations of program effectiveness may result. There may be a tendency, for example, to compare the amount of poverty in a community before a specific program was introduced with that of a few years later—and the reduction (if any) in poverty might be used as a measure of the program's effectiveness. The problem is that the program could have been enormously successful, while the prevalence of poverty in the community may have increased. Even a highly successful program in an urban slum area is much less likely to bring a disappearance of the slum than it is to bring an out-migration of the program's beneficiaries. The area might continue to be poverty-ridden, as beneficiaries of a successful program moved out only to be replaced by other poor people, particularly those who were eager to benefit from the added community services.

This last point poses another problem in project evaluation: there will be a tendency for a community with a successful but small-scale antipoverty program to attract those poor people who are most eager to take advantage of the opportunities—and most likely to benefit from them. A process of self-selection will be at work. Consequently, programs that are quite successful on a small scale may prove to be far less successful when attempted on a national scale, where the favorable self-selection will not operate.

CONCLUSION

Advice to policy-makers concerning antipoverty efforts is diverse and conflicting, as the articles below demonstrate. For Leon Keyserling, the antipoverty arsenal includes a very broad range of measures. But as Milton Friedman sees it, a simple program of cash grants (perhaps through the income-tax system) is the best way to help the poor. Moreover, he believes that public housing and minimum-wage laws—which have Keyserling's warm support—are actually intensifying poverty. Friedman is joined by Michael Harrington in his condemnation of existing housing programs. To Gunnar Myrdal, much poverty is a result of "structural" unemployment, necessitating programs of worker retraining and relocation; to Harry Johnson, fiscal and monetary stimulants are the key to solving the problem of unemployment. And to Irving Kristol, a simple and uncomplicated tax cut for low-income people would go far toward solving a problem which, it seems to him, has been exaggerated. Can we judge the validity of each position?

The problems of defining the goals of an antipoverty program and learning how to attain them at minimum cost in terms of other goals are many and difficult. But the stakes are high. The stakes are not merely the resources of a nation, but the lives of millions of people whose prospects for a better life for themselves and their children depend largely upon our learning more about poverty and effective devices for attacking it.

NOTES

1. Mollie Orshansky, "Counting the Poor: Another Look at the Poverty Profile," *Social Security Bulletin*, XXVIII (January 1965), 3-29.
2. In a later study this adjustment was reduced to 30 per cent. See Mollie Orshansky, "Who's Who Among the Poor: A Demographic View of Poverty," *Social Security Bulletin*, XXVIII (July 1965), 3-32.
3. Many of the data presented here refer to poor *families*. It should be remembered, however, that there are many poor persons living alone. In 1963 there were 4.9 million such "unrelated individuals" with incomes under $1500, the figure generally felt to be comparable to the $3000 figure for families. Of these, 70 per cent were women, and more than half were sixty-five years of age or older.

PART I

The Problem: Who Are the Poor, and Why Are They Poor?

SECTION A

The General Character of Poverty

THE INVISIBLE LAND

Michael Harrington

Michael Harrington's The Other America *was published in 1962 and quickly stirred public concern about poverty in the United States. This chapter from his book develops the theme that the American poor are physically, politically, and culturally isolated from the mainstream of American life, and have therefore been forgotten. Harrington, sometimes described as a social reformer, has been associate editor of* The Catholic Worker *and a contributing editor to* Dissent *and* New America.

There is a familiar America. It is celebrated in speeches and advertised on television and in the magazines. It has the highest mass standard of living the world has ever known.

In the 1950s this America worried about itself, yet even its anxieties were products of abundance. The title of a brilliant book was widely misinterpreted, and the familiar America began to call itself *the affluent society*. There was introspection about Madison Avenue and tailfins; there was discussion of the emotional suffering taking place in the suburbs. In all this, there was an implicit assumption that the basic grinding economic problems had been solved in the United States. In this theory the nation's problems were no longer a matter of basic human needs—of food, shelter, and clothing. Now they were seen as qualitative, a question of learning to live decently amid luxury.

While this discussion was carried on, there existed another America. In it dwelt somewhere between 40 million and 50 million citizens of this land. They were poor. They still are.

To be sure, the other America is not impoverished in the same sense as those poor nations where millions cling to hunger as a defense against starvation. This country has escaped such extremes. That does not change the fact that tens of millions of Americans are, at this very moment, maimed in body and spirit, existing at levels beneath those necessary for human decency. If these people are not starving, they are hungry, and sometimes fat with hunger, for that is what cheap foods do. They are without adequate housing and education and medical care.

The government has documented what this means to the bodies of the poor. . . . But even more basic, this poverty twists and deforms the spirit. The American poor are pessimistic and defeated, and they are victimized by mental suffering to a degree unknown in Suburbia.

This book is a description of the world in which these people live; it is about the other America. Here are the unskilled workers, the migrant farm workers, the aged, the minorities, and all the others who live in the economic underworld of American life. In all this, there will be statistics, and that offers the opportunity for disagreement among honest and sincere men. I would ask the reader to respond critically to every assertion, but not to allow statistical quibbling to obscure the huge, enormous, and intolerable fact of poverty in America. For, when all is said and done, that fact is unmistakable, whatever its exact dimensions, and the truly human reaction can only be outrage. As W. H. Auden wrote:

> *Hunger allows no choice*
> *To the citizen or the police;*
> *We must love one another or die.*

I

The millions who are poor in the United States tend to become increasingly invisible. Here is a great mass of people, yet it takes an effort of the intellect and will even to see them.

I discovered this personally in a curious way. After I wrote my first article on poverty in America, I had all the statistics down on paper. I had proved to my satisfaction that there were around 50 million poor in this country. Yet, I realized I did not believe my own figures. The poor existed in the government reports; they were percentages and numbers in long, close columns, but they were not part of my experience. I could prove that the other America existed, but I had never been there.

My response was not accidental. It was typical of what is happening to an entire society, and it reflects profound social changes in this nation. The other America, the America of poverty, is hidden today in a way that it never was before. Its millions are socially invisible to the rest of us. No wonder that so many misinterpreted Galbraith's title and assumed that *the affluent society* meant that everyone had a decent standard of life. The misinterpretation was true as far as the actual day-to-day lives of two thirds of the nation were concerned. Thus, one must begin a description of the other America by understanding why we do not see it.

There are perennial reasons that make the other America an invisible land.

Poverty is often off the beaten track. It always has been. The ordinary tourist never left the main highway, and today he rides interstate turnpikes. He does not go into the valleys of Pennsylvania where the towns look like movie sets of Wales in the 1930s. He does not see the company houses in rows, the rutted roads (the poor always have bad roads whether they live in the city, in towns, or on farms), and everything is black and dirty. And even if he were to pass through such a place by accident, the tourist would not meet the unemployed men in the bar or the women coming home from a runaway sweatshop.

Then, too, beauty and myths are perennial masks of poverty. The traveler comes to the Appalachians in the lovely season. He sees the hills, the streams, the foliage—but not the poor. Or perhaps he looks at a rundown mountain house and—remembering Rousseau rather than seeing with his eyes—decides that "those people" are truly fortunate to be living the way they are and that they are lucky to be exempt from the strains and tensions of the middle class. The only problem is that "those people," the quaint inhabitants of those hills, are undereducated, underprivileged, lack medical care, and are in the process of being forced from the land into a life in the cities, where they are misfits.

These are normal and obvious causes of the invisibility of the poor. They operated a generation ago; they will be functioning a generation hence. It is more important to understand that the very development of American society is creating a new kind of blindness about poverty. The poor are increasingly slipping out of the very experience and consciousness of the nation.

If the middle class never did like ugliness and poverty, it was at least aware of them. "Across the tracks" was not a very long way to go. There were forays into the slums at Christmas time; there were charitable organizations that brought contact with the poor. Occasionally, almost everyone passed through the Negro ghetto or the blocks of tenements, if only to get downtown to work or to entertainment.

Now the American city has been transformed. The poor still inhabit the miserable housing in the central area, but they are increasingly isolated from contact with, or sight of, anybody else. Middle-class women coming in from Suburbia on a rare trip may catch the merest glimpse of the other America on the way to an evening at the theater, but their children are segregated in suburban schools. The business or professional man may drive along the fringes of slums in a car or bus, but it is not an important experience to him. The failures, the unskilled, the disabled, the aged, and the minorities are right there, across the tracks, where they have always been. But hardly anyone else is.

In short, the very development of the American city has removed poverty from the living, emotional experience of millions upon millions of middle-class Americans. Living out in the suburbs, . . . [we find it] easy to assume that ours is, indeed, an affluent society.

This new segregation of poverty is compounded by a well-meaning ignorance. A good many concerned and sympathetic Americans are aware that there is much discussion of urban renewal. Suddenly, driving through the city, they notice that a familiar slum has been torn down and that there are towering, modern buildings where once there had been tenements or hovels. There is a warm feeling of satisfaction, of pride in the way things are working out: the poor, it is obvious, are being taken care of.

The irony in this . . . is that the truth is nearly the exact opposite to the impression. The total impact of the various housing programs in postwar America has been to squeeze more and more people into existing slums. More often than not, the modern apartment in a towering building rents at $40 a room or more. For, during the past decade and a half, there has been more subsidization of middle- and upper-income housing than there has been of housing for the poor.

Clothes make the poor invisible too: America has the best-dressed poverty the world has ever known. For a variety of reasons, the benefits of mass production have been spread much more evenly in this area than in many others. It is much easier in the United States to be decently dressed than it is to be decently housed, fed, or doctored. Even people with terribly depressed incomes can look prosperous.

This is an extremely important factor in defining our emotional and existential ignorance of poverty. In Detroit the existence of social classes became much more difficult to discern the day the companies put lockers in the plants. From that moment on, one did not see men in work clothes on the way to the factory, but citizens in slacks and white shirts. This process has been magnified . . . throughout the country. There are ten of thousands of Americans in the big cities who are wearing shoes, perhaps even a stylishly cut suit or dress, and yet are hungry. It is not a matter of planning, though it almost seems as if the affluent society had given out costumes to the poor so that they would not offend the rest of society with the sight of rags.

Then, many of the poor are the wrong age to be seen. A good number of them (over 8 million) are sixty-five years of age or better; an even larger number are under eighteen. The aged members of the other America are often sick, and they cannot move. Another group of them live out their lives in loneliness and frustration: they sit in rented rooms, or else they stay close to a house in a neighborhood that has completely changed from the old days. Indeed, one of the worst aspects of poverty among the aged is that these people are out of sight and out of mind, and alone.

The young are somewhat more visible, yet they too stay close to their neighborhoods. Sometimes they advertise their poverty through a lurid tabloid story about a gang killing. But generally they do not disturb the quiet streets of the middle class.

And finally, the poor are politically invisible. It is one of the cruelest ironies of social life in advanced countries that the dispossessed at the bottom of society are unable to speak for themselves. The people of the other America do not, by far and large, belong to unions, to fraternal organizations, or to political parties. They are without lobbies of their own; they put forward no legislative program. As a group, they are atomized. They have no face; they have no voice.

Thus, there is not even a cynical political motive for caring about the poor, as in the old days. Because the slums are no longer centers of powerful political organizations, the politicians need not really care about their inhabitants. The slums are no longer visible to the middle class, so much of the idealistic urge to fight for those who need help is gone. Only the social agencies have a really direct involvement with the other America, and they are without any great political power.

To the extent that the poor have a spokesman in American life, that role is played by the labor movement. The unions have their own particular idealism: an ideology of concern. More than that, they realize that the existence of a reservoir of cheap, unorganized labor is a menace to wages and working conditions throughout the entire economy. Thus, many union legislative proposals—to extend the coverage of minimum-wage [laws] and Social Security, to organize migrant farm laborers—articulate the needs of the poor.

That the poor are invisible is one of the most important things about them. They are not simply neglected and forgotten as in the old rhetoric of reform; what is much worse, they are not seen.

Forty to 50 million people are becoming increasingly invisible. That is a shocking fact. But there is a second basic irony of poverty that is equally important: if one is to make the mistake of being born poor, he should choose a time when the majority of the people are miserable too.

J. K. Galbraith develops this idea in *The Affluent Society* and, in doing so, defines the "newness" of the kind of poverty in contemporary America. The old poverty, Galbraith notes, was general. It was the condition of life of an entire society, or at least of that huge majority who were without special skills or the luck of birth. When the entire economy advanced, a good many of these people gained higher standards of living. Unlike the poor today, the majority poor of a generation ago were an immediate (if cynical) concern of political leaders. The old slums of the immigrants had the votes; they provided the basis for labor organiza-tions; their very numbers could be a powerful force in political conflict. At the same time the new technology required higher skills, more educa-tion, and stimulated an upward movement for millions.

Perhaps the most dramatic case of the power of the majority poor took place in the 1930s. The Congress of Industrial Organizations [CIO] literally organized millions in a matter of years. A labor movement that had been declining and confined to a thin stratum of the highly skilled suddenly embraced masses of men and women in basic industry. At the same time this acted as a pressure upon the government, and the New Deal codified some of the social gains in laws like the Wagner Act. The result was not a basic transformation of the American system, but it did transform the lives of an entire section of the population.

In the 1930s one of the reasons for these advances was that misery was general. There was no need then to write books about unemploy-ment and poverty. That was the decisive social experience of the entire society, and the apple-sellers even invaded Wall Street. There was po-litical sympathy from middle-class reformers; there were an acute *élan* and spirit that grew out of a deep crisis.

Some of those who advanced in the 1930s did so because they had unique and individual personal talents. But for the great mass, it was a question of being at the right point in the economy at the right time in history, and utilizing that position for [a] common struggle. Some of those who failed did so because they did not have the will to take advantage of new opportunities. But for the most part the poor who were left behind had been at the wrong place in the economy at the wrong moment in history.

These were the people in the unorganizable jobs, in the South, in the minority groups, in the fly-by-night factories that were low on capital and high on labor. When some of them did break into the economic mainstream—when, for instance, the CIO opened up the way for some Negroes to find good industrial jobs—they proved to be as resourceful as anyone else. . . . [The] Americans who stayed behind were not . . . primarily . . . individual failures; rather, they were victims of an impersonal process that selected some for progress and discriminated against others.

Out of the 1930s came the welfare state. Its creation had been stimulated by mass impoverishment and misery, yet it helped the poor least of all. Laws like unemployment compensation, the Wagner Act, the various farm programs—all these were designed for the middle third in the cities, for the organized workers, and for the upper third in the country, for the big market farmers. If a man works in an extremely low-paying job, he may not even be covered by Social Security or other welfare programs. If he receives unemployment compensation, the payment is scaled down according to his low earnings.

One of the major laws that was designed to cover everyone, rich and poor, was Social Security. But even here the other Americans suffered discrimination. Over the years Social Security payments have not even provided a subsistence level of life. The middle third have been able to supplement the federal pension through private plans negotiated by unions, through joining [such] medical-insurance schemes . . . [as] Blue Cross, and so on. The poor have not been able to do so. They lead a bitter life, and then have to pay for that fact in old age.

Indeed, the paradox that the welfare state benefits those least who need help most is but a single instance of a persistent irony in the other America. Even when the money finally trickles down—even when a school is built in a poor neighborhood, for instance—the poor are still deprived. Their entire environment, their life, their values, do not prepare them to take advantage of the new opportunity. The parents are anxious for the children to go to work; the pupils are pent up, waiting for the moment when their education has complied with the law.

Today's poor, in short, missed the political and social gains of the 1930s. They are, as Galbraith rightly points out, the first minority poor in history, the first poor not to be seen, the first poor whom the politicians could leave alone.

The first step toward the new poverty was taken when millions of people proved immune to progress. When that happened, the failure was not individual and personal, but a social product. But once the historic accident takes place, it begins to become a personal fate.

The new poor of the other America saw the rest of society move ahead. They went on living in depressed areas, and often they tended to become depressed human beings. In some of the West Virginia towns, for instance, an entire community will become shabby and defeated. The young and the adventurous go to the city, leaving behind those who cannot move and those who lack the will to do so. The entire area becomes permeated with failure, and that is one more reason the big corporations shy away.

Indeed, one of the most important things about the new poverty is that it cannot be defined in simple, statistical terms. . . . If a group has internal vitality, a will—if it has aspiration—it may live in dilapidated housing, it may . . . [have] an inadequate diet, and it may suffer poverty, but it is not impoverished. So it was in those ethnic slums of the immigrants that played such a dramatic role in the unfolding of the American dream. The people found themselves in slums, but they were not slum-dwellers.

But the new poverty is constructed so as to destroy aspiration; it is a system designed to be impervious to hope. The other America does not contain the adventurous seeking a new life and land. It is populated by the failures, by those driven from the land and bewildered by the city, by old people suddenly confronted with the torments of loneliness and poverty, and by minorities facing a wall of prejudice.

In the past, when poverty was general in the unskilled and semi-skilled work force, the poor were all mixed together. The bright and the dull, those who were going to escape into the great society and those who were to stay behind, all of them lived on the same street. When the middle third rose, this community was destroyed. And the entire invisible land of the other Americans became a ghetto, a modern poor farm for the rejects of society and of the economy.

It is a blow to reform and the political hopes of the poor that the middle class no longer understands that poverty exists. But, perhaps more important, the poor are losing their links with the great world. If statistics and sociology can measure a feeling as delicate as loneliness . . . , the other America is becoming increasingly populated by those who do not belong to anybody or anything. They are no longer participants in an ethnic culture from the old country; they are less and less religious; they do not belong to unions or clubs. They are not seen, and because of that they themselves cannot see. Their horizon has become more and more restricted; they see one another, and that means they see little reason to hope.

Galbraith was one of the first writers to begin to describe the newness of contemporary poverty, and that is to his credit. Yet because even he underestimates the problem, it is important to put his definition into perspective.

For Galbraith, there are two main components of the new poverty: case poverty and insular poverty. Case poverty is the plight of those who suffer from some physical or mental disability that is personal and individual and excludes them from the general advance. Insular poverty exists in areas like the Appalachians or the West Virginia coal fields, where an entire section of the country becomes economically obsolete.

Physical and mental disabilities are, to be sure, an important part of poverty in America. The poor are sick in body and in spirit. But this is not an isolated fact about them, an individual "case," a stroke of bad luck. Disease, alcoholism, low IQ's—these express a whole way of life. They are, in the main, the effects of an environment, not the biographies of unlucky individuals. Because of this, the new poverty is something that cannot be dealt with by first aid. If there is to be a lasting assault on the shame of the other America, it must seek to root out of this society an entire environment, and not just the relief of individuals.

But perhaps the idea of insular poverty is even more dangerous. To speak of "islands" of the poor (or, in the more popular term, of "pockets of poverty") is to imply that one is confronted by a serious, but relatively minor, problem. This is hardly a description of a misery that extends to 40 million or 50 million people in the United States. They have remained impoverished in spite of increasing productivity and the creation of a welfare state. That fact alone should suggest the dimensions of a serious and basic situation.

And yet, even given these disagreements with Galbraith, his achievement is considerable. He was one of the first to understand that there are enough poor people in the United States to constitute a subculture of misery, but not enough of them to challenge the conscience and the imagination of the nation.

Finally, one might summarize the newness of contemporary poverty by saying: these are the people who are immune to progress. But then the facts are even more cruel. The other Americans are the victims of the very inventions and machines that have provided a higher living standard for the rest of the society. They are upside-down in the economy, and for them greater productivity often means worse jobs; agricultural advance becomes hunger.

In the optimistic theory, technology is an undisguised blessing. A general increase in productivity, the argument goes, generates a higher standard of living for the whole people. And indeed, this has been true for the middle and upper thirds of American society, the people who made such striking gains in the last two decades. It tends to overstate the automatic character of the process, to omit the role of human struggle. (The CIO was organized by men in conflict, not by economic trends.) Yet it states a certain truth—for those who are lucky enough to participate in it.

But the poor, if they were given to theory, might argue the exact opposite. They might say: progress is misery.

As the society . . . [becomes] more technological, more skilled, those who learn to work the machines, who get expanding education, move up. Those who miss out at the very start find themselves at a new disadvantage. A generation ago in American life, the majority of the working people did not have high school educations. But at that time industry was organized on a lower level of skill and competence. And there was a sort of continuum in the shop: the youth who left school at sixteen could begin as a laborer, and gradually pick up skill as he went along.

Today the situation is quite different. The good jobs require much more academic preparation, much more skill from the very outset. Those who lack a high school education tend to be condemned to the economic underworld—to low-paying service industries, to backward factories, to sweeping and janitorial duties. If the fathers and mothers of the contemporary poor were penalized a generation ago for their lack of schooling, their children will suffer all the more. The very rise in productivity that created more money and better working conditions for the rest of the society can be a menace to the poor.

But then this technological revolution might have an even more disastrous consequence: it could increase the ranks of the poor as well as intensify the disabilities of poverty. At this point it is too early to make any final judgment, yet there are obvious danger signals. There are millions of Americans who live just the other side of poverty. When a recession comes, they are pushed onto the relief rolls. (Welfare payments in New York respond almost immediately to any economic decline.) If automation continues to inflict more and more penalties on the unskilled and the semiskilled, it could have the impact of permanently increasing the population of the other America.

Even more explosive is the possibility that people who participated in the gains of the 1930s and the 1940s will be pulled back down into poverty. Today the mass-production industries where unionization made such a difference are contracting. Jobs are being destroyed. In the process, workers who had achieved a certain level of wages, who had won [good] working conditions in the shop, are suddenly confronted with impoverishment. This is particularly true for anyone over forty years of age and for members of minority groups. Once their job[s are] . . . abolished, their chances of ever getting similar work are very slim.

It is too early to say whether or not this phenomenon is temporary, or whether it represents a massive retrogression that will swell the numbers of the poor. To a large extent, the answer to this question will be determined by the political response of the United States in the 1960s. If serious and massive action is not undertaken, it may be necessary for statisticians to add some old-fashioned, prewelfare-state poverty to the misery of the other America.

Poverty in the 1960s is invisible and it is new, and both these factors make it more tenacious. It is more isolated and politically powerless than ever before. It is laced with ironies, not the least of which is that many of the poor view progress upside-down—as a menace and a threat to their lives. And if the nation does not measure up to the challenge of automation, poverty in the 1960s might be on the increase.

II

There are mighty historical and economic forces that keep the poor down; and there are human beings who help out in this grim business, many of them unwittingly. There are sociological and political reasons why poverty is not seen; and there are misconceptions and prejudices that literally blind the eyes. The latter must be understood if anyone is to make the necessary act of intellect and will so that the poor can be noticed.

Here is the most familiar version of social blindness: "The poor are that way because they are afraid of work. And anyway they all have big cars. If they were like me (or my father or my grandfather), they could pay their own way. But they prefer to live on the dole and cheat the taxpayers."

This theory, usually thought of as a virtuous and moral statement, is one of the means of making it impossible for the poor ever to pay their way. There are, one must assume, citizens of the other America who choose impoverishment out of fear of work (though, writing it down, I really do not believe it). But the real explanation of why the poor are where they are is that they made the mistake of being born to the wrong parents, in the wrong section of the country, in the wrong industry, or in the wrong racial or ethnic group. Once that mistake has been made, they could have been paragons of will and morality, but most of them would never even have had a chance to get out of the other America.

There are two important ways of saying this: the poor are caught in a vicious circle; or: the poor live in a culture of poverty.

In a sense, one might define the contemporary poor in the United States as those who, for reasons beyond their control, cannot help themselves. All the most decisive factors making for opportunity and advance are against them. They are born going downward, and most of them stay down. They are victims whose lives are endlessly blown round and round the other America.

Here is one of the most familiar forms of the vicious circle of poverty. The poor get sick more than anyone else in the society. That is because they live in slums, jammed together under unhygienic conditions; they have inadequate diets, and cannot get decent medical care. When they become sick, they are sick longer than any other group in the society. Because they are sick more often and longer than anyone else, they lose wages and work, and find it difficult to hold a steady job. And because of this, they cannot pay for good housing, for a nutritious diet, for doctors. At any given point in the [cycle], particularly when there is a major illness, their prospect is to move to an even lower level and to begin the cycle, round and round, toward even more suffering.

This is only one example of the vicious circle. Each group in the other America has its own particular version of the experience, . . . but the pattern, whatever its variations, is basic to the other America.

The individual cannot usually break out of this vicious circle. Neither can the group, for it lacks the social energy and political strength to turn its misery into a cause. Only the larger society, with its help and resources, can really make it possible for these people to help themselves. Yet those who could make the difference too often refuse to act because of their ignorant, smug moralisms. They view the effects of poverty— above all, the warping of the will and spirit that is a consequence of being poor—as choices. Understanding the vicious circle is an important step in breaking down this prejudice.

There is an even richer way of describing this same, general idea: poverty in the United States is a culture, an institution, a way of life.

There is a famous anecdote about Ernest Hemingway and F. Scott Fitzgerald. Fitzgerald is reported to have remarked to Hemingway: "The rich are different." And Hemingway replied: "Yes, they have money." Fitzgerald had much the better of the exchange. He understood that being rich was not a simple fact, like a large bank account, but a way of looking at reality—a series of attitudes, a special type of life. If this is true of the rich, it is ten times truer of the poor. Everything about them—from the condition of their teeth to the way in which they love—is suffused and permeated by the fact of their poverty. And this is sometimes a hard idea for a Hemingway-like middle-class America to comprehend.

The family structure of the poor, for instance, is different from that of the rest of the society. There are more homes without a father, there is less marriage, more early pregnancy, and—if Kinsey's statistical findings can be used—markedly different attitudes toward sex. As a result of this, to take but one consequence of the fact, hundreds of thousands—and perhaps millions—of children in the other America never know stability and "normal" affection.

Or perhaps the policeman is an even better example. For the middle class, the police protect property, give directions, and help old ladies. For the urban poor, the police are those who arrest you. In almost any slum there is a vast conspiracy against the forces of law and order. If someone approaches asking for a person, no one there will have heard of him, even if he lives next door. The outsider is "cop," bill collector, investigator (and, in the Negro ghetto, most dramatically, he is "the Man").

While writing this book, I was arrested for participation in a civil-rights demonstration. A brief experience of a night in a cell made an abstraction personal and immediate: the city jail is one of the basic institutions of the other America. Almost everyone whom I encountered in the "tank" was poor: skid-row whites, Negroes, Puerto Ricans. Their poverty was an incitement to arrest in the first place. (A policeman will be much more careful with a well-dressed, obviously educated man who might have political connections than he will with someone who is poor.) They did not have money for bail or for lawyers. And, perhaps most important, they [a]waited their arraignment with stolidity, in a mood of passive acceptance. They expected the worst, and they probably got it.

There is, in short, a language of the poor, a psychology of the poor, a world view of the poor. To be impoverished is to be an internal alien, to grow up in a culture that is radically different from the one that dominates the society. The poor can be described statistically; they can be analyzed as a group. But they need a novelist as well as a sociologist if we are to see them. They need an American Dickens to record the smell and texture and quality of their lives. The cycles and trends, the massive forces, must be seen as affecting persons who talk and think differently.

. . . I work on an assumption that cannot be proved by government figures or even documented by impressions of the other America. It is an ethical proposition, and it can be simply stated: in a nation with a technology that could provide every citizen with a decent life, it is an outrage and a scandal that there should be such social misery. Only if one begins with this assumption is it possible to pierce through the invisibility of 40 million to 50 million human beings and to see the other America. We must perceive passionately, if this blindness is to be lifted from us. A fact can be rationalized and explained away; an indignity cannot.

What shall we tell the American poor, once we have seen them? Shall we say to them that they are better off than the Indian poor, the Italian poor, the Russian poor? That is one answer, but it is heartless. I should put it another way. I want to tell every well-fed and optimistic American that it is intolerable that so many millions should be maimed in body and in spirit when it is not necessary that they should be. My standard of comparison is not how much worse things used to be. It is how much better they could be if only we were stirred.

THE FACE OF ONE-FIFTH A NATION

Linda Lear

Linda Lear was a junior at the University of Kentucky and a vice chairman of the National Student YWCA when she wrote this article. In it, she tells of her experiences with poverty in the urban slums of Atlanta and New York City, where she worked for two summers.

I cannot say I am grateful for the experience of seeing the slums of Atlanta, Georgia, or those of New York City. It's a grand opportunity to broaden my awareness of life in these United States. But seeing poverty has sickened me, robbed me of the satisfaction of how good life is. Poverty is disturbing, ugly, and it drains my body of any sense of power or energy to change its conditions. I hurry away from its pathetic scenes like a child who pleaded to see a Frankenstein horror movie and after the show runs home to have her mother tell her it wasn't really true—"Don't believe it, it's all made up."

One wonderful thing about going into the slums is the satisfaction of knowing that you are going to get to come back out. It's like getting a shot in the arm. You only have to feel it hurt for a minute or so and then forget it. In the slums you only have to tolerate the smell of sewers, walk around trash and dog messes, talk to a few people, and explain to them that you are part of a study group seeking information and would like to ask them a few questions. After you feel you have a picture of the conditions in the slums you can leave.

Oh, is it a great relief! You don't feel stiff and uncomfortable any more and you can be off to a jolly good time or back to the comforts of your own home.

Poverty was not a reality for me until the summer of 1963. Growing up in a fairly prosperous farming community in southern Illinois, I can truly say I never really encountered poverty.

From *The Intercollegian* (December 1964). Reprinted by permission of the National Student Councils of the YMCA and YWCA.

43

The YWCA destroyed my optimistic outlook on life when I attended a 1963 summer conference in Atlanta, Georgia. Working with professional people in urban renewal, I learned the paradox of the big city. It is so easy for the splendor, charm, and graciousness of a southern city to over-shadow the hidden ugliness of slums that are only a few blocks from the state capitol. From the urban renewal workers I learned the complexity of their job—surveying neighborhoods, relocating tenants who must move because their so-called home is scheduled for slum clearance. They were to help frightened people find new homes. Those who were not eligible for federal housing units would flee to some other slum area in the city.

I went into homes with one of the social workers. In one case we met an eighty-four-year-old grandmother who was caring for her six grand-children. The mother of the children appeared only long enough to dump another baby off on the grandmother to care for. The oldest of the grandchildren, a girl of thirteen, had been missing for a week. The grandmother had asked the neighbors about the girl, but no one seemed to know much.

We went to this home to take the grandmother down to the office to apply for federal housing. Her three-year-old grandson came with us, a little boy named Fred. Fred had on a shirt and jeans, but was bare-footed. The moment he got in the car he started sucking his thumb. I teased him: "Hey, Fred, don't suck your thumb." When we got to the office I gave him a magazine with a picture of a collie dog on it. I looked over at him a few moments later and he was chewing on the pages of the magazine. Deciding maybe he was hungry, another girl and I took Fred down to the drug store and treated him to a vanilla milkshake. Fred liked it so much we finally had to take it away from him for fear he wouldn't breathe because he was sucking on the straw so hard. His grandmother was very pleased to learn he had had milk; he never got it at home.

While surveying slum areas, we passed a two-room shack where seven-teen people lived. They had to sleep in shifts and people were crowded on the porch in chairs.

Yes, I felt I had really had an encounter with poverty. I returned home to Illinois, where I spoke to Rotary Clubs and youth groups trying to arouse their concern.

Last summer I excitedly returned to the summer conference where I participated on a team that worked in slum housing in Buttermilk Bot-toms. Although this area is not the worst slum in Atlanta, it certainly has a name for its deplorable conditions. Weathered gray shacks were elevated above the ground on concrete blocks. There are many people living in the slums in Atlanta, but the slums seem more like a rural country area—which is a great contrast to the density . . . you find . . . in a single block in Harlem.

Buttermilk Bottoms supposedly got its name because of the condition of the place after a big rain. Needless to say, there are no front lawns, grass, or trees to absorb the moisture after a heavy rain and the water runs freely over the barren ground. The whole area becomes like a hog wallow with mud the consistency of buttermilk running between a person's toes. A social worker told me it was once necessary for him to wear hip boots when he went in this area after a heavy rain. Shacks line alleys that are often impassable by car.

We worked on our project of interviewing the people in this area in teams of interracial pairs. Buttermilk Bottoms was scheduled to be torn down and cleared so the property might be purchased by the city for a new auditorium. It was a pleasant thought to think of this area being leveled and beautified, but tragic in that the people living here must find new homes. We were concerned about these people and where they would go.

We . . . asked to see inside the homes so we might see if they met the housing code. Was there hot and cold running water[? Were there] screens on the windows, adequate plumbing facilities? We asked the people if they knew the area was scheduled to be cleared. Did they have any plans for where they would move? Were they sorry to leave?

It was so hard to talk to these people. It seemed we just couldn't get any real answers from them other than "Yes" and "I don't know." It wasn't that they were always withholding information; it was more a total lack of understanding the connection of our questions. As I think back over some of the questions we asked, I suppose they thought we were rather silly: "Why is there no effort around here to keep garbage picked up? Do you read the newspapers?" Here we were trying to categorize their lives by our standards. Yes, there was definitely a lack of communication. It got to be quite a strain on us to conduct these interviews.

We wanted to find out and offer an explanation for why these slum tenements were in such horrible condition. Who was responsible? The tenants weren't doing their part in caring for the property; the owners refused to repair rundown housing, saying the tenants would only tear it up again. The owner, in many cases, never sees the property he owns or never gets to know the people living on it. Instead he has a realtor collect the rent and supervise the property for him. How can this vicious circle be broken when all those involved fail to accept their responsibilities?

City officials told us that our generation would be the one to see that the conditions of poverty changed. They had become aware of the problem and were beginning to cope with it, but our generation must be the one to make the real changes. Hearing this only increased the despair and helplessness I felt. What were these poverty-stricken people to do while you and I and our generation slowly get around to facing the issue of these depressed people? And why after all this time did we have to be the people delegated to eradicate the whole horrible mess?

I wanted to take all the little children I saw in the slums home with me. Give them a bath, clean clothes, hold them on my lap, and read storybooks to them. How silly—and, oh, how impossible. If my contribution toward changing these conditions was to . . . [give] more talks, I didn't think I could stand it. I wanted to see changes made —action taken—and talk only seemed to draw one response: "My, Linda, what a wonderful experience for you to see these things!"

People, it wasn't wonderful; it was agonizing.

The week was over. I could leave poverty behind me. Thank God. I could go home. Somehow I found it very hard to stop thinking about all the little children, especially one tiny little Negro boy who cried and tugged at my hand to have the chewing gum in my mouth.

It wasn't long . . . [before] I found myself in New York City to attend Leadership Training School, with six weeks of study, culture, and entertainment before me.

One of the course requirements was to do a project in East Harlem, an area 50 per cent Puerto Rican, 40 per cent American Negro, and 10 per cent remnants of all previous immigrant groups. Here again were slums and poverty, only slightly different from anything I had seen before:

Fifteen-story dwellings with people looking out of windows, sheets and clean clothes dangling between buildings on sagging ropes to dry; the sidewalks crowded with people; women in tight dresses with protruding stomachs; girls with long, stringy hair and lots of eye make-up; children jumping rope or playing chase; men leaning against buildings or huddled in groups playing with dice; garbage cans lined up on the walk in front of each building; smells, bars, policemen, babies, bums, drunks, churches, and noise.

All these sights were new, exciting, and strange. Walking through the streets of Harlem and East Harlem, I experienced somewhat different feelings than in the slums of Atlanta. The people here in New York wore their anxieties on their faces, whereas in the South it seemed much harder to decide whether the people were so desperate they wouldn't talk or whether they were more content with living the way they were.

While working on my project in East Harlem, I assisted with a remedial reading program one afternoon. My job was to keep one problem child, José, from disrupting the rest of the school that was held in one room. José was a small Puerto Rican boy, about nine years old, who had very poor eyesight. He wore little horn-rimmed glasses, . . . one stem of . . . [which was] held on with a safety pin. He could not read any better than a first-grader and quickly lost interest in trying after a few sentences. José kept missing the word *let—l-e-t.* I sounded the word out for him, and then said, "José, you know what the word *let* means. You say to your older sister, 'Let me have the book.' "

José said, "Yeah, I say to her, 'Let me have it or I'll kick your ass off!' "

Well, the word finally had meaning for him, and he understood better than I had ever realized the force one could use when he said *let.*

Also, while working in East Harlem, we had an interview with one of the directors of the Narcotics Bureau. This office is a storefront right on the street. I was shocked when I learned that the employees of the bureau don't go in search of the narcotic addict; instead, they just open the front door and the addicts come pouring in. The director said on a winter afternoon as many as fifty people will come into the office for help.

"We actually have to hide sometimes and shut the door in their faces. We just can't give aid to alcoholics even though many of them come to us for help. We can't even minister to all the addicts who petition for our help. We have about six men coming in for help in comparison to one woman. This doesn't mean there aren't more women though; it's easier for the women to support their habit through prostitution. If a prostitute is fairly attractive she can easily take in about $100 a day. We don't do anything with the youths who are addicted; and, as far as I know, there is no organization that is especially concerned with the young addict. Very little success is . . . [to be achieved] with young people. It usually takes a few years for them to really want to break the habit."

This is pretty shocking, isn't it? It sounds like an exaggeration. Spend a day or two in the neighborhood—it's no joke.

What is the public attitude about slums? What is necessary to change this attitude? How can we expect the middle and upper classes who don't even have concern for their next-door neighbor[s] to care about the thousands of poor?

If we draw attention to poverty, the general public seems to accept it in two ways. Great amounts of sympathy are felt, but no action is taken to make changes. The other opinion seems to be: if the people in the slums want to get out of these conditions, they can—all they need is ambition and determination. In his book, *The Other America*, Michael Harrington says: "The people who are much too sensitive to ask cripples to run races turn around and require the poor to act like everybody else in society. It can't be done."

The vicious circle of poverty spins swiftly. No one can get out of it without somebody slowing it down. These people don't want sympathy; they need action.

In East Harlem I saw a drunkard curled up in a corner. In one hand was an empty whiskey bottle. His eyes were closed, his face was bloody red, and he lay in a puddle of his own urine.

Only a few feet away were half a dozen children playing jump rope and laughing. They seemed completely unaware of the drunken man. Of course they knew he was there. But scenes like this are so common that there was no reason for them to be excited or frightened; they have accepted the drunkard as a way of life.

This is the example they see around them. You and I grew up seeing people who succeeded and found meaning in life. But these children are nourished on failure and despair.

I don't really know of an efficient way to go about changing public opinion. But I would like to share a story that stresses the urgency of doing something about this problem.

I accompanied a group of kindergarten children from East Harlem to the Central Park Zoo. The teacher was making some last-minute comments to the children. Speaking to one little Puerto Rican girl, she asked: "What will you do if you get lost while we are at the zoo?" The little girl assuredly replied: "Get found."

I really believe that it is up to you and me and our generation to justify the faith that this child has in life. Will she get found before she becomes lost in the depths and darkness of poverty?

The question is before us. The decision must be made, I pray that God will impart to us wisdom, strength, and dedication as we face this issue.

THE NEW POSITION OF POVERTY

John Kenneth Galbraith

In this chapter from The Affluent Society, *John Kenneth Galbraith examines the anomaly of poverty amidst plenty. He concludes that poverty in the United States today is of two types:* case poverty, *resulting from some individual quality (such as mental deficiency or inadequate education), and* insular poverty, *resulting from unwillingness or inability to leave a chronically poor community. Such poverty, according to Galbraith, will not succumb to economic growth alone. Galbraith is Professor of Economics at Harvard University and author of such other books as* The Great Crash *and* The Liberal Hour. *He was U.S. Ambassador to India in the early 1960s.*

I

"The study of the causes of poverty," Alfred Marshall observed at the turn of the century, "is the study of the causes of the degradation of a large part of mankind." He spoke of contemporary England as well as of the world beyond. A vast number of people both in town and country, he noted, had insufficient food, clothing, and houseroom; they were: "Overworked and undertaught, weary and careworn, without quiet and without leisure." The chance of their succor, he concluded, gave to economic studies "their chief and their highest interest." [1]

No contemporary economist would be likely to make such an observation about the United States. Conventional economic discourse does make occasional obeisance to the continued existence of some poverty. "We must remember that we still have a great many poor people." This usefully allays uneasiness about the relevance of conventional economic goals and especially of economic efficiency. For some people wants must be synthesized. Hence the importance of the goods is not per se very high.

But others are far closer to need. And hence we must not be cavalier about the urgency of providing them with the most for the least. The sales tax may have merit for the opulent, but it still bears heavily on the poor. Thus poverty survives in economic discourse partly as a buttress to the conventional economic wisdom. Still, in a world of a weekly industrial wage of eighty dollars and a $3960 median family income, it can no longer be presented as a universal or massive affliction. It is more nearly an afterthought.

The privation of which Marshall spoke was, a half-century ago, the common lot at least of all who worked without special skill. As a general affliction, it was ended by increased output which, however imperfectly it may have been distributed, nevertheless accrued in substantial amount to those who worked for a living. The result was to reduce poverty from the problem of a majority to that of a minority. It ceased to be a general case and became a special case. It is this which has put the problem of poverty into its peculiar modern form.

II

For poverty does survive. There is no firm definition of this phenomenon and again, save as a tactic for countering the intellectual obstructionist, no precise definition is needed. In part it is a physical matter; those afflicted have such limited and insufficient food, such poor clothing, such crowded, cold, and dirty shelter that life is painful as well as comparatively brief. But just as it is far too tempting to say that, in matters of living standards, everything is relative, so it is wrong to rest everything on absolutes. People are poverty-stricken when their income, even if adequate for survival, falls markedly behind that of the community. Then they cannot have what the larger community regards as the minimum necessary for decency; and they cannot wholly escape, therefore, the judgment of the larger community that they are indecent. They are degraded for, in the literal sense, they live outside the grades or categories which the community regards as acceptable. In the mid-1950s, by acceptable estimate, one family in thirteen in the United States had a cash income from all sources of less than a thousand dollars. In addition, a very large number of individuals, not members of families, were in this income class. To some extent family life is itself a luxury of an adequate income. The hard core of the very poor was declining, but not with great rapidity.

A substantial share of these low incomes are in agriculture—in 1964, 27.4 per cent of all farm families had cash incomes of less than a thousand dollars as compared with 4.9 per cent of urban families who were below this level. These rural families had further incomes in the form of shelter and farm-grown food which causes the estimate of cash income to understate their position. However, there is probably more danger of exaggerating than of minimizing the contribution of the unpainted shacks, the reluctant animals, and the barren garden patches by which the rural poor eke out their income.

This agricultural poverty has a tendency to be concentrated in specific areas. The Appalachian plateau and its valleys, parts of the southern coastal plain and the Piedmont plateau, the country of low hills between the Appalachians and the Mississippi, the cutover lands of the [Great] Lake[s] states, the Ozark plateau, all provide examples. In 1950 in such areas nearly a million farm families had *gross* receipts of less than $1200 and about a quarter of a million had less than $250. In the southern Appalachians the average net income of *all* full-time farmers in 1949 was less than $500. In the southern Piedmont the average was only slightly higher. In 1950 1.5 million . . . farm families, principally in the abovementioned areas, had net cash incomes from all sources of less than a thousand dollars. The modern locus of poverty is even more the rural than the urban slum.

III

One can think of modern poverty as falling into two broad categories. First there is what may be called *case poverty.* This one encounters in every community, rural or urban, however prosperous that community or the times. Case poverty is the poor farm family with the junk-filled yard and the dirty children playing in the bare dirt. Or it is the gray-black hovel beside the railroad tracks. Or it is the basement dwelling in the alley.

Case poverty is commonly and properly related to some characteristic of the individuals so afflicted. Nearly everyone else has mastered his environment; this proves that it is not intractable. But some quality peculiar to the individual or family involved—mental deficiency, bad health, inability to adapt to the discipline of modern economic life, excessive procreation, alcohol, insufficient education, or perhaps a combination of several of these handicaps—have kept these individuals from participating in the general well-being.

Second, there is what may be called *insular poverty*—that which manifests itself as an "island" of poverty. In the island everyone or nearly everyone is poor. Here, evidently, it is not so easy to explain matters by individual inadequacy. We may mark individuals down as intrinsically deficient; it is not proper or even wise so to characterize an entire community. For some reason the people of the island have been frustrated by their environment.

This is not the place to explore in detail the causes of insular poverty. They are complex and many of the commonly assigned causes are either excessively simple or wrong. The resource endowment or the fertility of the land, the commonplace explanations, have little to do with it. Connecticut, a state of high incomes, has few resources and a remarkably stony soil. West Virginia is richly endowed. Connecticut has long been rich and West Virginia poor.

Insular poverty has something to do with the desire of a comparatively large number of people to spend their lives at or near the place of their birth. This homing instinct causes them to bar the solution, always open as an individual remedy in a country without barriers to emigration, to escape the island of poverty in which they were born. And so long as they remain they are committed to a pattern of agricultural land use or of mining, industrial, or other employment which is unproductive, episodic, or otherwise unremunerative.* Meanwhile the poverty of the community insures that educational opportunities will be limited, that health services will be poor, and that subsequent generations will be ill prepared either for mastering the environment into which they are born or for migration to areas of higher income outside. It is a reasonable presumption, too, that the homing instinct operates most powerfully among the poorly educated.

In some circumstances escape may not be possible. Especially in the urban slum, race or poverty may confine individuals to an area of intrinsically limited opportunity. And once again the environment perpetuates its handicaps through poor schools, evil neighborhood influences, and bad preparation for life.

The most certain thing about modern poverty is that it is not efficiently remedied by a general and tolerably well-distributed advance in income. Case poverty is not remedied because the specific individual inadequacy precludes employment and participation in the general advance. Insular poverty is not directly alleviated because the advance does not necessarily

---

* Thus in the Appalachian plateau, settlement occurred along the valleys on farms which were of the small scale appropriate to a largely self-sufficient agriculture. Time has rendered such agriculture obsolete. Other areas produce the same crops far more efficiently; changing standards have made what once seemed a tolerable standard of living exceedingly primitive. Yet the massive reorganization of land use that would be required—far larger farms or conceivably highly capitalized forest enterprises—are far beyond the capacities, both educational and financial, of the people involved. Meanwhile the homing instinct causes them—or at least, a large number—to persist in the area.

remove the specific frustrations of environment to which the people of these islands are subject. This is not to say that it has no effect. Secure job opportunities elsewhere, a concomitant of industrial advance, work against the homing instinct. And so even more directly does the spread of industrialization. The appearance of industry in parts of the Tennessee Valley area has had a strong remedial effect on the insular poverty of those areas. But it remains that advance cannot improve the position of those who, by virtue of self or environment, cannot participate or are not reached.

IV

These circumstances have caused a profoundly interesting although little recognized change in what may be termed the political economy of poverty. With the transition of the very poor from a majority to a comparative minority position, they ceased to be automatically an object of interest to the politician. Political identification with those of the lowest estate has anciently brought the reproaches of the well-to-do, but it has had the compensating advantage of alignment with a large majority. Now any politician who speaks for the very poor is speaking for a small and also inarticulate minority. As a result the modern liberal politician aligns himself not with the poverty-ridden members of the community but with the far more numerous people who enjoy the far more affluent income of (say) the modern trade union member. Ambrose Bierce, in *The Devil's Dictionary*, called poverty "a file provided for the teeth of the rats of reform." It is so no longer. Reform now concerns itself with people who are relatively well-to-do—whether the comparison be with their own past or with those who are really at the bottom of the income ladder.

The poverty-stricken are further forgotten because it is assumed that with increasing output poverty must disappear. Increased output eliminated the general poverty of all who worked. Accordingly it must, sooner or later, eliminate the special poverty that still remains. As we have just seen, this is not to be expected or, in any case, it will be an infinitely time-consuming and unreliable remedy. Yet just as the arithmetic of modern politics makes it tempting to overlook the very poor, so the supposition that increasing output will remedy their case has made it easy to do so too.

To put the matter another way, the concern for inequality had vitality only so long as the many suffered privation while a few had much. It did not survive as a burning issue in a time when the many had much even though others had much more. It is our misfortune that when inequality declined as an issue, the slate was not left clean. A residual and in some ways rather more hopeless problem remained.

V

An affluent society, that is also both compassionate and rational, would, no doubt, secure to all who needed it the minimum income essential for decency and comfort. The corrupting effect on the human spirit of a small amount of unearned revenue has unquestionably been exaggerated as, indeed, have the character-building values of hunger and privation. To secure to each family a minimum standard, as a normal function of the society, would help insure that the misfortunes of parents, deserved or otherwise, were not visited on their children. It would help insure that poverty was not self-perpetuating. Most of the reaction, which no doubt would be almost universally adverse, is based on obsolete attitudes. When poverty was a majority phenomenon, such action could not be afforded. A poor society . . . had to enforce the rule that the person who did not work could not eat. And possibly it was justified in the added cruelty of applying the rule to those who could not work or whose efficiency was far below par. An affluent society has no similar excuse for such rigor. It can use the forthright remedy of providing for those in want. Nothing requires it to be compassionate. But it has no high philosophical justification for callousness.

Nonetheless any such forthright remedy for poverty is beyond reasonable hope. Also, as in the limiting case of the alcoholic or the mental incompetent, it involves difficulties. To spend income requires a minimum of character and intelligence even as to produce it. By far the best hope for the elimination, or in any case the minimization, of poverty lies in less direct but, conceivably, almost equally effective means.

The first and strategic step in an attack on poverty is to see that it is no longer self-perpetuating. This means insuring that the investment in children from families presently afflicted be as little below normal as possible. If the children of poor families have first-rate schools and school attendance is properly enforced; if the children, though badly fed at home, are well nourished at school; if the community has sound health services, and the physical well-being of the children is vigilantly watched; if there is opportunity for advanced education for those who qualify regardless of means; and if, especially in the case of urban communities, law and order are well enforced and recreation is adequate—then there is a very good chance that the children of the very poor will come to maturity without grave disadvantage. In the case of insular poverty this remedy requires that the services of the community be assisted from outside. Poverty is self-perpetuating because the poorest communities are poorest in the services which would eliminate it. To eliminate poverty efficiently we should invest more than proportionately in the children of the poor community. It is there that high-quality schools, strong health services, special provision for nutrition and recreation are most needed to compensate for the very low investment which families are able to make in their own offspring.

The effect of education and related investment in individuals is to enable them either to contend more effectively with their environment, or to escape it and take up life elsewhere on more or less equal terms with others. The role of education as an antidote to the homing instinct which crowds people into the areas of inadequate opportunity and frustration is also clear. However, in the strategy of the attack on insular poverty, a place remains for an attack on the frustrations of the environment itself. This is particularly clear in the case of the slum. Slum clearance and expansion of low- and middle-income housing removes a comprehensive set of frustrations and greatly widens opportunity. There is a roughly parallel opportunity in the rural slum. By identifying a land use which is consistent with a satisfactory standard of living, and by assisting with the necessary reorganization of land and capital, public authority can help individuals to surmount frustrations to which they are now subject. The process promises to be expensive and also time-consuming. But the question is less one of feasibility than of will.

Nor is case poverty in the contemporary generation wholly intransigent. Much can be done to treat those characteristics which cause people to reject or be rejected by the modern industrial society. Educational deficiencies can be overcome. Mental deficiencies can be treated. Physical handicaps can be remedied. The limiting factor is not knowledge of what can be done. Overwhelmingly it is our failure to invest in people.

VI

It will be clear that to a remarkable extent the requirements for the elimination of poverty are the same as for social balance. (Indeed a good deal of case poverty can be attributed to the failure to maintain social balance.) The myopic preoccupation with production and material investment has diverted our attention from the more urgent questions of how we are employing our resources and, in particular, from the greater need and opportunity for investing in persons.

Here is a paradox. When we begin to consider the needs of those who are now excluded from the economic system by accident, inadequacy, or misfortune, we find that the normal remedy is to make them or their children productive citizens. This means that they add to the total output of goods. We see once again that even by its *own terms* the present pre-occupation with material as opposed to human investment is inefficient. The parallel with investment in the supply of trained and educated man-power . . . will be apparent.

But increased output of goods is not the main point. Even to the most intellectually reluctant reader it will now be evident that enhanced pro-ductive efficiency is not the *motif* of this volume. The very fact that in-creased output offers itself as a byproduct of the effort to eliminate poverty is one of the reasons. No one would be called upon to write at such length on a problem so easily solved as that of increasing produc-tion. The main point lies elsewhere. Poverty—grim, degrading, and in-eluctable—is not remarkable in India. For few the fate is otherwise. But in the United States the survival of poverty is remarkable. We ignore it because we share with all societies at all times the capacity for not see-ing what we do not wish to see. Anciently this has enabled the nobleman to enjoy his dinner while remaining oblivious to the beggars around his door. In our own day it enables us to travel in comfort through south Chicago and the South. But while our failure to notice can be explained, it cannot be excused. "Poverty," Pitt exclaimed, "is no disgrace but it is damned annoying." In the contemporary United States it is not annoying, but it is a disgrace.

NOTES

1. Alfred Marshall, *Principles of Economics,* 8th ed. (New York: The Macmillan Company, 1920), pp. 2-4.

THE FUTURE OF THE LOW-INCOME PROBLEM

Robert J. Lampman

Are the poor immune to economic growth? This is the subject of the concluding chapter of Robert J. Lampman's study, The Low-Income Population and Economic Growth. *Lampman participated actively in the development of the Administration's antipoverty program as a member of the* CEA *staff and, later, as a consultant to the* CEA *and the* OEO. *He is Professor of Economics at the University of Wisconsin, author of* The Share of Top Wealthholders in National Wealth, 1922-56, *and editor of* Social Security Perspectives.

WILL THE REDUCTION OF POVERTY BE SLOWER IN THE FUTURE?

It is argued by some that the future rate of change will be slower because present-day poverty is qualitatively different from the poverty found in earlier days. Whereas oldtime poverty was general, the new poverty, it is alleged, is specific and associated with a limited number of groups. These groups are, in turn, said to be those which are not likely to be improved by a generalized type of national economic growth because they are "immune" to such progress. This immunity arises out of personal characteristics or an environment which insulates them from opportunities for earning higher income.

Prof[essor] John Kenneth Galbraith, in his book, *The Affluent Society,* writes of three kinds of poverty: namely, generalized poverty, island poverty, and case poverty. The first is the kind which yields to the process of economic growth in which the average productivity of labor is increased. The latter two, he asserts, are the principal kinds of poverty remaining in the United States today and these are caused respectively by inability or unwillingness to move out of low-income areas or regions, and

From *The Low-Income Population and Economic Growth,* by Robert J. Lampman, Study Paper No. 12, United States Congress, Joint Economic Committee, 1959.

. . . some quality peculiar to the individual or family involved—mental deficiency, bad health, inability to adapt to the discipline of modern economic life, excessive procreation, alcohol, insufficient education, or perhaps a combination of several of these handicaps. . . .

Galbraith states that in the early 1950s "The hard core of the very poor was declining, but not with great rapidity." Further, he argues:

The most certain thing about modern poverty is that it is not efficiently remedied by a general and tolerably well-distributed advance in income. Case poverty is not remedied because the specific individual inadequacy precludes employment and participation in the general advance. Insular poverty is not directly alleviated because the advance does not necessarily remove the specific frustrations of environment to which the people of these islands are subject. This is not to say it has no effect. Secure job opportunities elsewhere, a concomitant of industrial advance, work against the homing instinct. And so, even more directly, does the spread of industrialization. The appearance of industry in parts of the Tennessee Valley area has had a strong remedial effect on the insular poverty of those areas. But it remains that advance cannot improve the position of those who, by virtue of self or environment, cannot participate or are not reached.

EVALUATION OF THE GALBRAITH THESIS

We submit that Professor Galbraith has misinterpreted the low-income problem in several ways. In the first place, our finding that the percent[age] of the total population in low income status fell from 26 to 19 per cent in ten years would seem to contradict—or, at least, not to confirm—his statement that "the hard core of the very poor was declining but not with great rapidity." In the second place, with regard to island poverty, the record suggests that movement was a leading factor working for the reduction of numbers in low income status. For instance, the number of rural farm families with under $2000 income (1947 dollars) actually fell during the 1947-57 period * from 3.3 to 2.4 million because of movement off the farm. Similarly, there were great shifts among occupations and industries which contributed to the reduction of low income units. Third, with respect to "case poverty," it should be pointed out that some of these characteristics of persons are moderated over time. For example, average educational attainment levels will rise in future years simply because younger people presently have better education than older people. Hence, as the current generation of old people

* EDITOR'S NOTE: Galbraith's *The Affluent Society* was published in 1958.

pass[es] from the scene, the percent[age] of persons with low educational attainment will fall.

Whether the reduction of low incomes . . . [resulting from] such improved levels of educational attainment should be attributed to economic growth or to social policy is a semantic problem. It is part of the adaptation to new and higher skill occupations and hard to separate from the whole process of growth. This process, in turn, pulls people into areas where educational opportunities are greater. This is not to deny that increased educational opportunity will not in itself contribute to the rate of growth.

. . . [Also,] we would take exception to Professor Galbraith's list of causal variables since he excludes the important ones of age, color, and sex of head.

Suppose now we take up the question as Galbraith implicitly, if quite awkwardly, puts it. Which groups among the contemporary low-income population are likely to diminish in the future, assuming a rising average level of income, and which ones are not likely to diminish? Do the answers to these questions suggest a slowing down of the rate at which we have been reducing the share of the population in low-income status?

WHAT GROUPS DO NOT BENEFIT BY ECONOMIC GROWTH?

It is true, of course, that some groups will not benefit from the process of growth in the same ways that others do. Those who are outside of the labor force tend to have an immunity to growth. (Here we are ignoring property income. Those who hold equity claims will tend to share in the growth of the economy thereby, even though they may be out of the labor force.) Those who cannot or will not move or change occupation, or who cannot otherwise adapt to changes in the economic environment, will run a greater risk of low-income status at some time in their lives than will others. In general, consumer unit heads who are least mobile and adaptable are seen to have a handicapping characteristic such as old age, nonwhite color, female sex, or low education. Old age is a handicap in the sense that older people typically have greater difficulty in getting re-employed than do younger people and in getting into new and rapidly growing occupations and industries. (In one sense, the aged group may be said to participate in growth if average old-age insurance and assistance payments rise with average income of the community. To the extent that the formula for computing old-age, survivors' and disability insurance benefits accounts for rising average monthly wages, those benefits will rise over time.) Nonwhite color is a handicap to the extent that color is a bar to higher income occupations. Female sex also operates to limit occupational choice and even, to some extent, geographic mobility. Low education limits mobility and adaptability by barring entry to and perhaps limiting knowledge of and motivation toward new occupational possibilities.

It is significant that the contemporary low-income population is disproportionately made up of persons having one or more of these characteristics. . . . [Although] about 50 per cent of the total population have one or more of the four handicapping characteristics, 70 per cent of the low-income population of 32.2 million persons had one or more of these characteristics.

There is plausibility in the idea that each one of these characteristics has causal significance in determining the numbers in low-income status. As we have already mentioned, one can confidently predict that the numbers having low educational attainment will fall and from that deduce that the percent[age] of persons having low income will fall.

. . . [Although] low educational attainment will diminish in importance over time, the other three "handicapping" characteristics of old age, nonwhite status, and female headship will not.

From this investigation of Galbraith's claim that "modern poverty" will not yield to general economic growth, we conclude—for reasons quite different from his—that there is limited validity to his claim and that the future rate of reduction in the percent[age] of the population in low-income status will tend to be slightly slower than in the recent past.

LOW-INCOME GROUP'S SHARE OF INCOME

All of this thinking about extending past experience assumes that the lowest-income groups will not increase their share of total income. The only way for their income to rise faster than the income of the rest of the population is, of course, for them to get a larger share of the total. To make faster progress in eliminating poverty than the above calculations suggest would require such an increasing share of income.

The lowest fifth of income receivers now get 5 per cent of all income. It received 5 per cent of income in 1947. It apparently received about 5 per cent of income in the 1930s. However, there has been some progress because the lowest fifth of income receivers (families and unattached individuals) now includes a smaller part of all persons than it once did. But no matter how one figures it, the change in share of income has not

been great. In general we have been overcoming poverty more by raising the general level of income than by increasing the share of the bottom
fifth at the expense of upper-income groups.

CHANGES IN ECONOMIC INEQUALITY

There is evidence for the belief that the distribution of income and
wealth are less unequal now than in earlier days. But the greatest part
of the change seems to have occurred within the top half of the distribution. That is, the top group's share has been lowered at the expense of a
gain in share by the upper middle group. Two leading studies into
changes of the size distribution of income have established that a noteworthy fall in the income share of the top 5 per cent of income receivers
took place between 1939 and 1945. Prof[essor] Simon Kuznets found
that the top 5 per cent of persons' share of disposable income fell from
27 to 18 per cent, or well over three-tenths.[1] Dr. Selma Goldsmith and
colleagues found a similar fall in the share of the top 5 per cent of
families in personal income.[2]

A study by the present author into the share of wealth held by top
wealthholders offers the finding of a gradual loss of share of wealth by
topranking persons and families.[3] Between 1922 and 1953 the top 2 per
cent of families' (ranked by size of wealth holdings) share of wealth fell
from 33 per cent to 29 per cent. However, it is found that the concentration of wealth is increasing in the years since 1949. The lesser fall in
inequality of wealth than in inequality of personal income calls attention
to the fact that disposable personal income has changed more in its
distribution than has national income.[4] Apparently the top-income group
has been able to offset its losses on income account to some extent by
gaining on capital account. This has occurred in large part through
corporate saving.

GOVERNMENT POLICY TOWARD INEQUALITY

These changes toward less inequality of wealth and income are apparently in some part . . . [the result of] the workings of "the market"
and private responses to economic changes. They are also in some part
. . . [the result of] government policies and programs. Principal among
these government activities are education, health, and welfare service
programs which improve the ability and motivation of poorer persons
to compete in the marketplace. Also important are tax and money-transfer
programs. Several studies have been made which confirm the fact that

over-all taxing and spending policies of federal, state, and local governments operate to diminish the inequality which arises in the market. Comparison of the over-all tax systems of prewar and postwar years suggests that the historical trend is, while very moderate indeed, toward a more equalizing tax system. In both the depression period and the postwar period the combined tax burden of the lowest fifth of consumer units has been heavy; about 19 per cent of their income going to taxes of all kinds in 1938-39 and about 25 per cent in 1948-54. The tax burden on the top fifth in the same period moved from 22 per cent to 34 per cent. The relative tax burden on the lowest fifth of consumer units is perhaps overstated in the more recent period because of the structural changes in the composition of that group. In short, the lower fifth of units has come to contain a smaller part of the total population with less of the nation's total of consumer needs than it once did.

In the same period government transfer payments have become a more important part of the income of the lowest fifth of consumer units. According to the Survey of Consumer Finances, about half the spending units in the lowest fifth received some transfer payments and transfer payments were 40 per cent of the total money income of the group. It seems clear that both the composition of this group and its share of income would be very different were it not for the tremendous growth of social insurance and related programs in recent years. In the last thirty years government transfer payments have increased from 1 per cent to 5 per cent of national income.

POSSIBILITIES FOR THE FUTURE

It is concluded, then, that progress in the elimination of poverty has been made with only a minor change in the share of income and wealth in the hands of the lowest fifth of consumer units. Continuation of past policies and past experience for another generation (thirty years) or so may be expected to result in the virtual elimination of what may reasonably (by present standards) be thought of as "low-income status." On the other hand, a relaxation in the rate of economic growth or a drop in the rate of increase of government transfer programs could make the goal of eliminating poverty recede into the far distant future. A higher rate of growth in average incomes, or a more aggressive government policy aimed at increasing the post-tax, post-transfer share of total income received by the lowest fifth of consumer units (or a combination of both growth and wide sharing), could lead to this result in less than a generation.

NOTES

1. "Shares of Upper-Income Groups in Income and Savings" (New York: National Bureau of Economic Research, 1953), p. xxxvii.
2. Selma F. Goldsmith, *et al.*, "Size Distribution of Income Since the Mid-Thirties," *Review of Economics and Statistics* (February 1954).
3. *Review of Economics and Statistics* (November 1959).
4. Selma F. Goldsmith, "Change in the Size Distribution of Income," *American Economic Review* (May 1957), p. 506.

The Measurement and Interpretation of Poverty

THE PROBLEM OF POVERTY IN AMERICA

Council of Economic Advisers

The CEA, *established by the Employment Act of 1946, presents an annual report to the President on the state of the economy and the outlook for it, and also advises the President on economic policy. In this chapter from the January 1964 Annual Report, the* CEA *presented an analysis of the magnitude and causes of poverty in the United States. The chapter continues to be an often-quoted source of data about the poor, while the measure of poverty used by the* CEA—$3000 *of money income per family—remains the subject of debate. The chairman of the* CEA *at that time was Walter W. Heller; the members were Gardner Ackley and John P. Lewis.*

In his message on the State of the Union, President Johnson declared all-out war on poverty in America. This chapter is designed to provide some understanding of the enemy and to outline the main features of a strategy of attack.

ELIMINATING POVERTY—A NATIONAL GOAL

There will always be some Americans who are better off than others. But it need not follow that "the poor are always with us." In the United States today we can see on the horizon a society of abundance, free of much of the misery and degradation that have been the age-old fate of man. Steadily rising productivity, together with an improving network of private and social insurance and assistance, has been eroding mass poverty in America. But the process is far too slow. It is high time to redouble and to concentrate our efforts to eliminate poverty.

From the *Economic Report of the President Together With the Annual Report of the Council of Economic Advisers,* January 1964.

Poverty is costly not only to the poor but to the whole society. Its ugly byproducts include ignorance, disease, delinquency, crime, irresponsibility, immorality, indifference. None of these social evils and hazards will, of course, wholly disappear with the elimination of poverty. But their severity will be markedly reduced. Poverty is no purely private or local concern. It is a social and national problem.

But the overriding objective is to improve the quality of life of individual human beings—for poverty deprives the individual not only of material comforts but of human dignity and fulfillment. Poverty is rarely a builder of character.

The poor inhabit a world scarcely recognizable, and rarely recognized, by the majority of their fellow Americans. It is a world apart, whose inhabitants are isolated from the mainstream of American life and alienated from its values. It is a world where Americans are literally concerned with day-to-day survival—a roof over their heads, where the next meal is coming from. It is a world where a minor illness is a major tragedy, where pride and privacy must be sacrificed to get help, where honesty can become a luxury and ambition a myth. Worst of all, the poverty of the fathers is visited upon the children.

Equality of opportunity is the American dream, and universal education our noblest pledge to realize it. But, for the children of the poor, education is a handicap race; many are too ill prepared and ill motivated at home to learn at school. And many communities lengthen the handicap by providing the worst schooling for those who need the best.

Although poverty remains a bitter reality for too many Americans, its incidence has been steadily shrinking. The fruits of general economic growth have been widely shared; individuals and families have responded to incentives and opportunities for improvement; government and private programs have raised the educational attainments, housing standards, health, and productivity of the population; private and social insurance has increasingly protected families against loss of earnings . . . [resulting from] death, disability, illness, old age, and unemployment. Future headway against poverty will likewise require attacks on many fronts: the active promotion of a full-employment, rapid-growth economy; a continuing assault on discrimination; and a wide range of other measures to strike at specific roots of low income. As in the past, progress will require the combined efforts of all levels of government and of private individuals and groups.

All Americans will benefit from this progress. Our nation's most precious resource is its people. We pay twice for poverty: once in the production lost in wasted human potential, again in the resources diverted to coping with poverty's social byproducts. Humanity compels our action, but it is sound economics as well.

This chapter considers, first, the changing numbers and composition of America's poor. Second, it presents a brief report on the factors that contribute to the continuation of poverty amidst plenty. Although the analysis is statistical, the major concern is with the human problems that the numbers reflect. The concluding part concerns strategy against poverty in the 1960s and beyond. . . .

The sections below will chart the topography of poverty. A few significant features of this bleak landscape deserve emphasis in advance. Poverty occurs in many places and is endured by people in many situations; but its occurrence is nonetheless highly concentrated among those with certain characteristics. The scars of discrimination, lack of education, and broken families show up clearly from almost any viewpoint. Here are some landmarks:

—One fifth of our families and nearly one fifth of our total population are poor.

—Of the poor, 22 per cent are nonwhite; and nearly one half of all nonwhites live in poverty.

—The heads of over 60 per cent of all poor families have only grade school educations.

—Even for those denied opportunity by discrimination, education significantly raises the chance to escape from poverty. Of all nonwhite families headed by a person with eight years or less of schooling, 57 per cent are poor. This . . . falls to 30 [per cent] for high school graduates and to 18 per cent for those with some college education.

—But education does not remove the effects of discrimination: when nonwhites are compared with whites at the same level of education, the nonwhites are poor about twice as often.

—One third of all poor families are headed by a person over sixty-five, and almost one half of families headed by such a person are poor.

—Of the poor, 54 per cent live in cities, 16 per cent on farms, 30 per cent as rural nonfarm residents.

—Over 40 per cent of all farm families are poor. More than 80 per cent of nonwhite farmers live in poverty.

—Less than half of the poor are in the South; yet a Southerner's chance of being poor is roughly twice that of a person living in the rest of the country.

—One quarter of poor families are headed by a woman; but nearly one half of all families headed by a woman are poor.

—When a family and its head have several characteristics frequently associated with poverty, the chances of being poor are particularly high: a family headed by a young woman who is nonwhite and has less than an eighth-grade education is poor in 94 out of 100 cases. Even if she is white, the chances are 85 out of 100 that she and her children will be poor.

THE NATURE AND EXTENT OF POVERTY

Measurement of poverty is not simple, either conceptually or in practice. By *the poor* we mean those who are not now maintaining a decent standard of living—those whose basic needs exceed their means to satisfy them. A family's needs depend on many factors, including the size of the family, the ages of its members, the condition of their health, and their place of residence. The ability to fulfill these needs depends on current income from whatever source, past savings, ownership of a home or other assets, and ability to borrow.

Needs and Resources

There is no precise way to measure the number of families who do not have the resources to provide minimum satisfaction of their *own* particular needs. . . . [Because] needs differ from family to family, an attempt to quantify the problem must begin with some concept of average need for an average or representative family. Even for such a family, society does not have a clear and unvarying concept of an acceptable minimum. By the standards of contemporary American society, most of the population of the world is poor; and most Americans were poor a century ago. But for our society today, a consensus on an approximate standard can be found. One such standard is suggested by a recent study, described in a publication of the Social Security Administration, which defines a "low-cost" budget for a nonfarm family of four and finds its cost in 1962 to have been $3955. The cost of what the study defined as an "economy-plan" budget was $3165. Other studies have used different market baskets, many of them costing more. On balance, they provide support for using as a boundary, a family whose annual money income from all sources was $3000 (before taxes and expressed in 1962 prices). This is a weekly income of less than $60.

These budgets contemplate expenditures of one third of the total on food—i.e., for a $3000 annual budget for a four-person family about $5 per person per week. Of the remaining $2000, a conservative estimate for housing (rent or mortgage payments, utilities, and heat) would be another $800. This would leave only $1200—less than $25 a week—for clothing, transportation, school supplies and books, home furnishings and supplies, medical care, personal care, recreation, insurance, and everything else. Obviously it does not exaggerate the problem of poverty to regard $3000 as the boundary.

A family's ability to meet its needs depends not only on its money income but also on its income in kind, its savings, its property, and its ability to borrow. But the detailed data (of the [U.S.] Bureau of the Census) available for pinpointing the origins of current poverty in the United States refer to money income. Refined analysis would vary the income cutoff by family size, age, location, and other indicators of needs and costs. This has not been possible. However, a variable income cutoff was used in the sample study of poverty in 1959 conducted at the University of Michigan Survey Research Center. This study also estimates the over-all incidence of poverty at 20 per cent; and its findings concerning the sources of poverty correspond closely with the results based on an analysis of Census data.

A case could be made, of course, for setting the over-all income limit either higher or lower than $3000, thereby changing the statistical measure of the size of the problem. But the analysis of the sources of poverty, and of the programs needed to cope with it, would remain substantially unchanged.

No measure of poverty as simple as the one used here would be suitable for determining eligibility for particular benefits or participation in particular programs. Nevertheless, it provides a valid benchmark for assessing the dimensions of the task of eliminating poverty, setting the broad goals of policy, and measuring our past and future progress toward their achievement.

If it were possible to obtain estimates of total incomes—including nonmoney elements—for various types of families, those data would be preferable for the analysis which follows. The Department of Commerce does estimate total nonmoney incomes in the entire economy in such forms as the rental value of owner-occupied dwellings and food raised and consumed on farms, and allocates them to families with incomes of different size. Because of statistical difficulties, these allocations are necessarily somewhat arbitrary, and are particularly subject to error for the lower-income groups. No attempt is made to allocate them by other characteristics that are meaningful for an analysis of poverty. Of course, the total of money plus nonmoney income that would correspond to the limit used here would be somewhat higher than $3000.

The Changing Extent of Poverty

There were 47 million families in the United States in 1962. Fully 9.3 million, or one fifth of these families—comprising more than 30 million persons—had total money incomes below $3000. Over 11 million of these family members were children, one sixth of our youth. More than 1.1 million families are now raising four or more children on such an income. Moreover, 5.4 million families, containing more than 17 million persons, had total incomes below $2000. More than a million children were being raised in very large families (six or more children) with incomes of less than $2000.

Serious poverty also exists among persons living alone or living in non-family units such as boarding houses. In 1962, 45 per cent of such "unrelated individuals" (5 million persons) had incomes below $1500, and 29 per cent (or more than 3 million persons) had incomes below $1000. . . . Thus, by the measures used here, 33-35 million Americans were living at or below the boundaries of poverty in 1962—nearly one fifth of our nation.

The substantial progress made since World II in eliminating poverty is shown . . . Table 1. In the decade 1947-56, when incomes were growing relatively rapidly, and unemployment was generally low, the number of poor families ([those] with incomes below $3000 in terms of 1962 prices) declined from 11.9 million to 9.9 million, or from 32 per cent to 23 per cent of all families. But in the period from 1957 through 1962, when total growth was slower and unemployment substantially higher, the number of families living in poverty fell less rapidly—to 9.3 million, or 20 per cent of all families.

The progress made since World War II has not involved any major change in the distribution of incomes. The one fifth of families with the highest incomes received an estimated 43 per cent of total income in 1947 and 42 per cent in 1962. The one fifth of families with the lowest incomes received 5 per cent of the total in 1947 and 5 per cent in 1963.

Even if poverty should hereafter decline at the relatively more rapid rate of the 1947-56 period, there would still be 10 per cent of the nation's families in poverty in 1980. And, if the decline in poverty proceeded at the slower rate achieved from 1957 on, 13 per cent of our families would still have incomes under $3000 in 1980. We cannot leave the further wearing away of poverty solely to the general progress of the economy. A faster reduction of poverty will require that the lowest fifth of our families be able to earn a larger share of national output.

TABLE 1.

Money income of families, 1947 and 1950-62

Year	Median money income of all families (1962 prices)		Percentage of families with money income	
	Dollars	Index, 1947 = 100	Less than $3000 (1962 prices)	Less than $2000 (1962 prices)
1947	4117	100	32	18
1950	4188	102	32	19
1951	4328	105	29	17
1952	4442	108	28	17
1953	4809	117	26	16
1954	4705	114	28	17
1955	5004	122	25	15
1956	5337	130	23	14
1957	5333	130	23	14
1958	5329	129	23	14
1959	5631	137	22	13
1960	5759	140	21	13
1961	5820	141	21	13
1962	5956	145	20	12

Sources: U.S. Department of Commerce and CEA.

THE COMPOSITION OF TODAY'S POOR

To mount an attack on poverty, we must know how to select our targets. Are the poor concentrated in any single geographical area? Are they confined to a few easily identifiable groups in society? Conclusions drawn from personal observation are likely to be misleading. Some believe that most of the poor are found in the slums of the central city, while others believe that they are concentrated in areas of rural blight. Some have been impressed by poverty among the elderly, while others are convinced that it is primarily a problem of minority racial and ethnic groups. But objective evidence indicates that poverty is pervasive. To be sure, the inadequately educated, the aged, and the nonwhite make up substantial portions of the poor population. But as Table 2 shows, the poor are found among all major groups in the population and in all parts of the country. . . .

TABLE 2.

Selected characteristics of all families and of poor families, 1962

Selected characteristic	Number of families (millions)		Percentage of total	
	All families	Poor families	All families	Poor families
Total	47.0	9.3	100	100
Age of head:				
14-24 years	2.5	.8	5	8
25-54 years	30.4	3.9	65	42
55-64 years	7.3	1.4	16	15
65 years and over	6.8	3.2	14	34
Education of head:*				
8 years or less	16.3	6.0	35	61
9-11 years	8.6	1.7	19	17
12 years	12.2	1.5	26	15
More than 12 years	9.3	.7	20	7
Sex of head:				
Male	42.3	7.0	90	75
Female	4.7	2.3	10	25
Labor force status of head:**				
Not in civilian labor force	8.4	4.1	18	44
Employed	36.9	4.6	78	49
Unemployed	1.7	.6	4	6
Color of family:				
White	42.4	7.3	90	78
Nonwhite	4.6	2.0	10	22
Children under 18 years of age in family:				
None	18.8	4.9	40	52
One to three	22.7	3.3	48	36
Four or more	5.5	1.1	12	11
Earners in family:				
None	3.8	2.8	8	30
One	21.1	4.3	45	46
Two or more	22.1	2.2	47	23
Regional location of family:† ††				
Northeast	11.5	1.6	25	17
North Central	13.1	2.3	29	25
South	13.5	4.3	30	47
West	7.0	1.0	16	11
Residence of family:†† ‡				
Rural farm	3.3	1.5	7	16
Rural nonfarm	9.9	2.7	22	30
Urban	31.9	5.0	71	54

* Based on 1961 income (1962 prices).
** Labor force status relates to survey week of March 1963.
† Based on 1960 residence and 1959 income (1962 prices).
†† Data are from 1960 Census and are therefore not strictly comparable with the other data shown in this table, which are derived from *Current Population Reports*.
‡ Based on 1959 residence and 1959 income (1962 prices).
NOTE: Data relate to families and exclude unrelated individuals. Poor families are defined as all families with total money income of less than $3000.
Sources: U.S. Department of Commerce and CEA.

Using the income measure of poverty described above, we find that 78 per cent of poor families are white. Although one third of the poor families are headed by a person sixty-five years old and over, two fifths are headed by persons in the twenty-five-to-fifty-four-year range. Although it is true that a great deal of poverty is associated with lack of

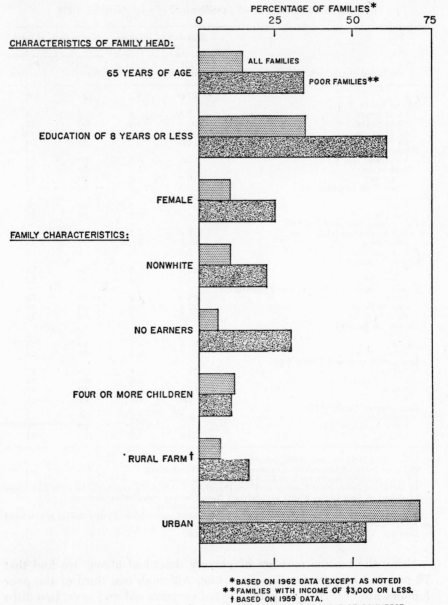

Characteristics of Poor Families
COMPARED WITH ALL FAMILIES

PERCENTAGE OF FAMILIES*

0   25   50   75

CHARACTERISTICS OF FAMILY HEAD:

65 YEARS OF AGE
ALL FAMILIES
POOR FAMILIES**

EDUCATION OF 8 YEARS OR LESS

FEMALE

FAMILY CHARACTERISTICS:

NONWHITE

NO EARNERS

FOUR OR MORE CHILDREN

RURAL FARM†

URBAN

*BASED ON 1962 DATA (EXCEPT AS NOTED)
**FAMILIES WITH INCOME OF $3,000 OR LESS.
†BASED ON 1959 DATA.
SOURCE: U.S. DEPARTMENT OF COMMERCE.

education, almost 4 million poor families (39 per cent) are headed by a person with at least some education beyond grade school. The data show that less than half the poor live in the South. And the urban poor are somewhat more numerous than the rural poor. In Chart 1, the poor and the nonpoor are compared in terms of these and other characteristics.

Yet there are substantial concentrations of poverty among certain groups. For example, families headed by persons sixty-five years of age and older represent 34 per cent of poor families. Moreover, they appear among the poor two and one-half times as frequently as they appear among all families. The last two columns of Table 2 show five additional major categories of families that appear more than twice as often among the poor as among the total population: nonwhite families, families headed by women, families headed by individuals not in the civilian labor force, families with no wage earners, and rural farm families. Of course, some of these groups overlap considerably; but the data help to identify prospective targets for an antipoverty attack. The next section pinpoints these targets further.

THE ROOTS OF POVERTY

Poverty is the inability to satisfy minimum needs. The poor are those whose resources—their income from all sources, together with their asset holdings—are inadequate. This section considers why those in poverty lack the earned income, property income and savings, and transfer payments to meet their minimum needs.

Earned Income

Why do some families have low earned incomes? Some are unemployed or partially unemployed. High over-all employment is a remedy of first importance. It would provide earned income for those unemployed who are able to accept jobs and greater earnings for many presently working part-time. Yet it is clear that this is only a partial answer. Even for those able and willing to work, earnings are all too frequently inadequate, and a large number of the poor are unable to work. An analysis of the incidence of poverty helps one understand the reasons for low earnings.

The *incidence* of poverty for any specified group of families is the percentage of that group with incomes below $3000. For all families, the incidence in 1962 was 20 per cent. An incidence for a particular group higher than 20 per cent, or higher than the rates for other similar groups, suggests that some characteristics of that group are causally related to poverty. The basic cause may not be the particular characteristic used to classify the group. But an examination of groups with high incidence should throw light on the roots of poverty. . . .

Table 4 shows that the incidence of poverty is 76 per cent for families with no earners. From other data, it appears that the incidence rate is 49 per cent for families headed by persons who work part-time. A family may be in either of these situations as a result of age, disability, premature death of the principal [wage] earner, need to care for children or disabled family members, lack of any salable skill, lack of motivation, or simply heavy unemployment in the area.

The problem of another group of families is the low rates of pay found most commonly in certain occupations. For example, the incidence of poverty among families headed by employed persons is 45 per cent for farmers, and 74 per cent for domestic service workers. . . .

The chief reason for low rates of pay is low productivity—which, in turn, can reflect lack of education or training, physical or mental disability, or poor motivation. Other reasons include discrimination, low bargaining power, exclusion from minimum-wage coverage, or lack of mobility resulting from inadequate knowledge of other opportunities, or unwillingness or inability to move away from familiar surroundings.

The importance of education as a factor in poverty is suggested by the fact that families headed by persons with no more than eight years of education have an incidence rate of 37 per cent (Table 3). Nonwhite and rural families show an even higher incidence of poverty (Table 3 . . .). The heads of these families are typically less well educated than average. For example, nonwhite family heads have completed a median of 8.7 years of school, compared to 11.8 for whites. In 1959 the median education of all males over twenty-five with incomes below $1000 and living on a farm was slightly above seven years in school; those with incomes above $5000 had completed over ten years in school.

. . . The severely handicapping influence of lack of education is clear. The incidence of poverty drops as educational attainments rise for nonwhite as well as white families at all ages. The high frequency of poverty for nonwhites is not, however, fully explained by their educational deficit. . . . [T]he incidence of poverty among nonwhites is almost invariably higher than among whites regardless of age, family type, or level of educational attainment. . . . [N]onwhites earn less than whites with the same education even when they practice the same occupation.

Some families are forced into poverty by society's own standards. Their potential earners, otherwise able to hold a job, cannot free themselves from the family responsibilities which they must fulfill. Such is the

TABLE 3.

Incidence of poverty by education, color, and residence, 1962

Selected characteristic	Incidence of poverty (per cent)
All families	20
Education of head:*	
8 years or less	37
9-11 years	20
12 years	12
More than 12 years	8
Color of family:	
White	17
Nonwhite	44
Residence of family:	
Farm	43
Nonwhite	84
Nonfarm	18

* Data relate to 1961, and money income in 1962 prices.

NOTE: Data relate to families and exclude unrelated individuals. Poverty is defined to include all families with total money income of less than $3000; these are also referred to as poor families. The incidence of poverty is measured by the percentage that poor families with a given characteristic are of all families having the same characteristic.

Sources: U.S. Department of Commerce and CEA.

case, for example, with families headed by women with small children.

Customary or mandatory retirement at a specified age also limits earnings by some healthy, able-bodied persons. However, retirement is often associated with deteriorating health, and poverty among the aged is greatest at ages over seventy or seventy-five and for aged widows—persons for whom employment is not a realistic alternative.

Property Income and Use of Savings

Some families with inadequate current earnings from work can avoid poverty thanks to past savings—which provide an income and, if necessary, can be used to support consumption. Savings are particularly important for the elderly. More than half of those over sixty-five have money incomes above $3000, and many also own homes. Others, although their money incomes are below $3000, have adequate savings that can be drawn upon to support a decent standard of consumption.

But most families with low earnings are not so fortunate. If avoiding poverty required an income supplement of $1500 a year for a retired man and his wife, they would need a capital sum at age sixty-five of about $19000 to provide such an annuity. Few families have that sum. The median net worth for all spending units (roughly equivalent to the total of families and unrelated individuals) was only $4700 in 1962. For all spending units whose head was sixty-five years or more, the median net worth was $8000. Meeting contingencies caused by illnesses is often a crucial problem for older people. About half of the aged, and about three fourths of the aged poor, have no hospital insurance, although their medical care costs are two and one half times as high as those of younger persons. Their resources are typically inadequate to cover the costs of a serious illness.

The median net worth of the fifth of all spending units having the lowest incomes was only $1000. Much of what property they have is in the form of dwellings. About 40 per cent of all poor families have some equity in a house. Although this means that their housing costs are reduced, property in this form does not provide money income that can be used for other current expenses.

Most families—including the aged—whose incomes are low in any one year lack significant savings or property because their incomes have always been at poverty levels. This is clear in the results of the Michigan study already cited. Among the reporting families classified in that study as poor in 1959, 60 per cent had never earned disposable income as high as $3000, and nearly 40 per cent had never reached $2000. The comparable figures for all families were 17 per ent and 10 per cent, respectively. Among the aged poor reporting, 79 per cent had never reached $3000, and fully one half had never earned $2000. While nearly 60 per cent of *all* families have enjoyed peak incomes above $5000, among all poor families only 14 per cent had ever reached that level; and a mere 5 per cent of the aged poor had ever exceeded $5000.

The persistence of poverty is reflected in the large number who have been unable to accumulate savings. The Survey Research Center study found that more than one half of the aged poor in 1959 had less than $500 in liquid savings (bank deposits and readily marketable securities), and they had not had savings above that figure during the previous five years. Less than one fifth of all poor families reported accumulated savings in excess of $500. The mean amount of savings used by poor families in 1959 was $120; and only 23 per cent of the poor drew on savings at all.

It is clear that for most families property income and savings do not provide a buffer against poverty. . . .

Transfer Payments and Private Pensions

Poverty would be more prevalent and more serious if many families and individuals did not receive transfer payments. In 1960, these payments (those which are not received in exchange for current services) constituted only 7 per cent of total family income, but they comprised 43 per cent of the total income of low-income spending units. At the same time, however, only about half of the present poor receive any transfer payments at all. And, of course, many persons who receive transfers through social-insurance programs are not poor—often as a result of these benefits.

Transfer programs may be either public or private in nature and may or may not have involved past contributions by the recipient. Public transfer programs include social insurance—such as unemployment compensation, workmen's compensation, and old-age, survivors', and disability insurance (OASDI); veterans' benefits; and public assistance programs, such as old age assistance (OAA) and aid to families with dependent children (AFDC).

Private transfer programs include organized systems such as private pension plans and supplementary unemployment benefits, organized private charities, and private transfers within and among families.

It is important to distinguish between insurance-type programs and assistance programs, whether public or private. Assistance programs are ordinarily aimed specifically at the poor or the handicapped. Eligibility for their benefits may or may not be based upon current income; but neither eligibility nor the size of benefits typically bears any direct relationship to past income. Eligibility for insurance-type programs, on the other hand, is based on past employment, and benefits on past earnings.

The federal-state unemployment insurance system covers only about 77 per cent of all paid employment and is intended to protect workers with a regular attachment to the labor force against temporary loss of income. Benefits, of course, are related to previous earnings.

. . . [Although] the largest transfer-payment program, OASDI, now covers approximately 90 per cent of all paid employment, there are still several million aged persons who retired or whose husbands retired or died before acquiring coverage. Benefits are related to previous earnings, and the average benefit for a retired worker under this program at the end of 1963 was only $77 a month, or $924 a year. The average benefit for a retired worker and his wife if she is eligible for a wife's benefit is $1565 a year.

Public insurance-type transfer programs have made notable contributions to sustaining the incomes of those whose past earnings have been adequate, and to avoiding their slipping into poverty as their earnings are interrupted or terminated. These programs are of least help to those whose earnings have never been adequate.

Public assistance programs are also an important support to low-income and handicapped persons. Money payments under OAA average about $62 a month for the country as a whole, with state averages ranging from $37 to about $95 a month. In the AFDC program the national average payment per family (typically of four persons) is about $129 a month, including services rendered directly. State averages range from $38 a month to about $197 a month.

Private transfers within and between families are included in the total money-income figures used in this chapter only to the extent that they are regular in nature—e.g., alimony or family-support payments, and are excluded when they take the form of casual or irregular gifts or bequests. . . . [Although] data are lacking on the value of such gifts, they are clearly not a major source of income for the poor.

Private pensions, providing an annuity, are additional resources for some persons and families. In 1961 the beneficiaries of such plans numbered about 2 million (as against about 12 million receiving OASDI benefits), and total benefits paid were about $2 billion. . . . [Although] the combination of OASDI and private pensions serves to protect some from poverty, most persons receiving OASDI receive no private pension supplement. In any case, benefits under private pension plans range widely, and since they are typically related to the individual's previous earnings, they are low when earnings have been low.

Thus, although many families do indeed receive supplements to earnings in the form of pensions, social-insurance benefits, and incomes from past saving, those families with a history of low earnings are also likely to have little of such supplementary income. And since most poor families have small amounts of property, they cannot long meet even minimum needs by depleting their assets.

The Vicious Circle

Poverty breeds poverty. A poor individual or family has a high probability of staying poor. Low incomes carry with them high risks of illness;

limitations on mobility; limited access to education, information, and training. Poor parents cannot give their children the opportunities for better health and education needed to improve their lot. Lack of motivation, hope, and incentive is a more subtle but no less powerful barrier than lack of financial means. Thus the cruel legacy of poverty is passed from parents to children.

Escape from poverty is not easy for American children raised in families accustomed to living on relief. A recent sample study of AFDC recipients found that more than 40 per cent of the parents were themselves raised in homes where public assistance had been received. It is difficult for children to find and follow avenues leading out of poverty in environments where education is deprecated and hope is smothered. This is particularly true when discrimination appears as an insurmountable barrier. Education may be seen as a waste of time if even the well-trained are forced to accept menial labor because of their color or nationality.

The Michigan study shows how inadequate education is perpetuated from generation to generation. Of the families identified as poor in that study, 64 per cent were headed by a person who had had less than an eighth-grade education. Of these, in turn, 67 per cent had fathers who had also gone no further than eighth grade in school. Among the children of these poor families who had finished school, 34 per cent had not gone beyond the eighth grade; this figure compares with 14 per cent for all families. Fewer than one in two children of poor families had graduated from high school, compared to almost two out of three for all families.

Of 2 million high school seniors in October 1959 covered by a Census study, 12 per cent did not graduate in 1960. Of these dropouts, 54 per cent had IQ's above 90, and 6 per cent were above 110. Most of them had the intellectual capabilities necessary to graduate. The dropout rate for nonwhite male students, and likewise for children from households with a nonworking head, was *twice* the over-all rate. And it was twice as high for children of families with incomes below $4000 as for children of families with incomes above $6000. Moreover, many of the children of the poor had dropped out before reaching the senior year.

A study of dropouts in New Haven, Connecticut, showed that 48 per cent of children from lower-class neighborhoods do not complete high school. The comparable figure for better neighborhoods was 22 per cent.

Other studies indicate that unemployment rates are almost twice as high for dropouts as for high school graduates aged sixteen–twenty-four. Moreover, average incomes of male high school graduates are 25 per cent higher than those of high school dropouts, and nearly 150 per cent

higher than those of men who completed less than eight years of schooling.

There is a well-established association between school status and
juvenile delinquency. For example, in the New Haven study cited above,
48 per cent of the dropouts, but only 18 per cent of the high school
graduates, had one or more arrests or referrals to juvenile court.

Low-income families lose more time from work, school, and other
activities than their more fortunate fellow citizens. Persons in families
with incomes under $2000 lost an average of eight days of work in the
year 1960-61, compared to 5.4 for all employed persons. They were restricted in activity for an average of thirty days (compared to 16.5 for
the whole population) and badly disabled for 10.4 days (compared to
5.8 for the whole population).

Recent Changes in the Pattern of Poverty

In spite of tendencies for poverty to breed poverty, a smaller proportion of our adult population has been poor—and a smaller fraction of
American children exposed to poverty—in each succeeding generation.
But, at least since World War II, the speed of progress has not been
equal for all types of families, as is shown in Table 4.

The incidence of poverty has declined substantially for most categories
shown in the table. But there are some notable exceptions—families with
no earner, [families] with head not in the civilian labor force, [families]
with head sixty-five years of age or older, [families] headed by a woman,
and [families] on farms. It is also striking that in these classes poverty
is high as well as stubborn. Poverty continues high also among nonwhites, although there has been a large and welcome decline in this
incidence.

With the sole exception of the farm group, the total number of *all*
families in each of these categories has remained roughly the same or
has increased. Hence the high-incidence groups, including the nonwhites,
have come to constitute a larger *proportion* of the poor (Table 5).

This tabulation shows that certain handicapping characteristics, notably old age, or absence of an earner or of a male family head, have
become increasingly prominent in the poor population. This is both a
measure of past success in reducing poverty and of the tenacity of the
poverty still existing. Rising productivity and earnings, improved education, and the structure of Social Security have permitted many families
or their children to escape; but they have left behind many families who

TABLE 4.

Number of families and incidence of poverty, by selected family characteristics,
1947 and 1962

Selected characteristic	Number of families			Incidence of poverty (percentage*)		Percentage change in number of poor families, 1947-62
	1947	1962	Percentage change, 1947 to 1962	1947	1962	
	Millions					
All families	37.3	47.0	26	32	20	−22
Earners in family:						
None	2.2	3.8	68	83	76	54
One	21.9	21.1	−4	35	20	−45
Two	9.9	17.0	73	20	10	−13
Three or more	3.3	5.1	56	10	8	29
Labor force status of head:**						
Not in civilian labor force	5.5	8.4	52	61	50	23
Unemployed	1.2	1.7	49	49	34	2
Employed	31.9	36.9	16	28	12	−48
Age of head:						
14-24 years	1.8	2.5	39	45	31	−6
25-54 years	25.0	30.4	22	27	13	−41
55-64 years	6.1	7.3	19	32	19	−28
65 years and over	4.4	6.8	54	57	47	27
Sex of head:						
Male	33.5	42.3	26	30	17	−30
Female	3.8	4.7	26	51	48	19
Color of family:						
White	34.2	42.4	24	29	17	−27
Nonwhite	3.1	4.6	46	67	44	−3
Children under 18 years of age in family:						
None	16.2	18.8	16	36	26	−16
One	8.9	8.7	−2	30	17	−46
Two	6.4	8.5	33	27	13	−33
Three or more	5.7	10.9	92	32	17	2
Regional location of family:†						
Northeast	10.1	11.5	14	26	14	−42
North Central	11.5	13.1	14	30	18	−31
South	11.5	13.5	17	49	32	−24
West	5.1	7.0	37	28	15	−26
Residence of family:						
Farm††	6.5	3.2	−51	56	43	−62
Nonfarm‡	30.8	43.8	42	27	18	−5

* The incidence of poverty is measured by the percentage that poor families with a given characteristic are of all families having the same characteristic.
** Labor force status is for April survey week of 1949 and March survey week of 1963. Income data (1962 prices) are for 1948 and 1962.
† Income data for 1949 and 1959. Since regional location data are from 1950 and 1960 Censuses, they are not strictly comparable with other data shown in this table, which are derived from *Current Population Reports.*
†† The 1960 Census change in definition of a farm resulted in a decline of slightly over 1 million in the total number of farm families. Therefore, the incidence figures for 1947 and 1962 may not be strictly comparable.
‡ Since 1959, nonfarm data are not available separately for rural nonfarm and urban.
NOTE: Data relate to families and exclude unrelated individuals. Poverty is defined to include all families with total money income of less than $3000 (1962 prices); these are also referred to as poor families.
Sources: U.S. Department of Commerce and CEA.

TABLE 5.

Selected characteristics of poor families, 1947 and 1962

	Percentage of poor families with characteristic	
Selected characteristic	1947	1962
Family head:		
65 years of age and over	20	34
Female	16	25
Nonwhite families	18	22
Rural farm families	30	20*
No earners in family	16	30

* Data are from *Current Population Reports* and are for 1959, based on income in 1962 prices. See Table 4, footnote †† for comparability problem.

NOTE: Data relate to families and exclude unrelated individuals. Poor families are defined as all families with total money income of less than $3000 (1962 prices).

Sources: U.S. Department of Commerce and CEA.

have one or more special handicaps. These facts suggest that in the future economic growth alone will provide relatively fewer escapes from poverty. Policy will have to be more sharply focused on the handicaps that deny the poor fair access to the expanding incomes of a growing economy.

But the significance of these shifts in composition should not be exaggerated. About half of the poor families are still headed neither by an aged person nor by a woman, and 70 per cent include at least one earner. High employment and vigorous economic growth are still of major importance for this group. And it is essential to remember that one third of the present poor are children. For them, improvements in the availability and quality of education offer the greatest single hope of escaping poverty as adults.

SOME ECONOMIC TASKS OF THE GREAT SOCIETY

Council of Economic Advisers

During the year following publication of its chapter on poverty in the 1964 Annual Report, the CEA attempted to fill some gaps in knowledge about the poor. Of special significance in this section from the 1965 Annual Report are data on the persistence of poverty among particular families over a two-year period. The CEA included Gardner Ackley, Chairman, and Otto Eckstein and Arthur M. Okun, Members.

Last year, the Council's Annual Report set forth a preliminary analysis of the structure of poverty, focusing on the economic characteristics of the poor and the causes of their poverty. Since then additional information has become available, shedding more light on the process by which family poverty may arise, persist, or disappear.

THE RECORD OF PROGRESS AGAINST POVERTY

The percentage of American families with incomes (in 1962 prices) below $3000 fell from 32 per cent in 1947 to 20 per cent in 1962 and to 19 per cent in 1963. Experience indicates that in periods of strong economic expansion the incidence of poverty declines. Between 1947 and 1962 the number of poor families fell from 11.9 million to 9.3 million; in 1963 alone it dropped an additional 300,000, and a further reduction probably occurred last year. The composition of this group of families showed little change from 1962 to 1963. The incidence of poverty remained highest among farm families, nonwhites, and those headed by females, and among the elderly, the least educated, and those unable to work. The median money income of poor families has remained close to $1800 since 1958.

From the *Economic Report of the President Together With the Annual Report of the Council of Economic Advisers,* January 1965.

MEASURES AND CHARACTERISTICS OF POVERTY

In its 1964 Annual Report, the Council proposed an income below $3000 as a test of family poverty. It recognized that a determination of poverty status cannot be exact, either conceptually or in practice, for "there is no precise way to measure the number of families who do not have the resources to provide minimum satisfaction of their *own* particular needs." However, the attack on poverty requires a quantitative perspective on the problem. Therefore, the Council concluded that the $3000 income limit "provides a valid benchmark for assessing the dimensions of the task of eliminating poverty, setting the broad goals of policy, and measuring our past and future progress toward their achievement."

In the past year, additional research has been devoted to measuring the character and extent of poverty, taking into account a broader range of considerations than annual income alone. This will permit the development of more comprehensive measures of the problem.

Differences in family composition

The $3000 poverty line was intended to reflect the minimum current income needs of a typical family—typical with respect to size, age of members, and a variety of other characteristics. Recognizing that few families are typical, the Social Security Administration has now estimated the income needed to achieve comparable minimum standards of consumption by families of various size and age composition in both rural and urban areas. The minimum income needs of an urban family of six, for example, will normally differ from those of an elderly rural couple.

Under these revised estimates, roughly the same total number of persons are classified poor as under the simpler $3000 family-income test, but the composition of the poverty group is somewhat different. The number of poor families is smaller; the number of adults is reduced, especially among the aged and those who do not work. The number of large families classified as poor increases, however; and, most important, the estimated number of children in poverty rises by more than one third—from 11 million to 15 million. This means that one fourth of the nation's children live in families that are poor. These findings underscore the importance of helping young people escape from poverty. This pressing objective, stressed in last year's Annual Report, is emphasized in the Economic Opportunity Act and in the President's new proposals for education and health care of children.

Asset ownership

A family's ability to maintain an adequate standard of living depends on its accumulation of assets and liabilities as well as [on its] current income. A family may be able to sustain its consumption during an occasional year of low income by drawing down savings, borrowing on assets, and postponing the replacement of durable goods. Thus the measurement of poverty is improved by distinguishing temporary from chronic inadequacy of income, and considering the asset holdings of low-income families. However, in practice, few low-income families can long maintain satisfactory consumption levels by drawing down their assets. Average (median) net asset holdings of poor families amounted to only $2760 at the end of 1962. The bulk of these assets consisted of equity in a home and thus could not be easily converted into consumption. Even if a typical poor family were to draw down its assets to supplement current income in order to maintain consumption at the rate of $3000 a year, these assets would be entirely exhausted within two to three years.

Older families with incomes of less than $3000 generally possess more assets than do younger families with low incomes. Many of the former are retired and are using their savings to meet living costs. A composite measure of poverty based upon income and asset criteria would exclude some older families now classified as poor under the income test alone.

Income variability and the persistence of poverty

The extent of chronic poverty is reflected by a measure of persistence —the percentage of poor families in any given year who remain poor in succeeding years. A study of incomes of the same families in two successive years shows that approximately 70 per cent with incomes below $3000 in one year have similarly low incomes in the following year. This suggests that the poor include a largely unchanging group of families. Persistence of poverty is greatest among families headed by females, the less educated, nonwhites, and the aged, as shown in Table 1.

Temporary poverty is likely to arise from unemployment, illness, or other disability, and—for the self-employed—from the hazards of small business. Movement out of poverty is related to changing levels of economic activity.

The process by which over-all poverty is reduced from one year to the next involves a number of divergent influences. Some families become poor, a slightly larger number become better off, but the great majority

TABLE 1.

*Persistence of poverty, by selected family
characteristics, 1962-63*

Selected characteristic	Persistence of poverty
All families	69
Age of head:	
14-24 years	62
25-34 years	55
35-44 years	53
45-54 years	63
55-64 years	71
65 years and over	80
Work experience of head:	
Worked	60
At full-time jobs	53
At full-year jobs*	51
At part-time jobs	79
Did not work	83
Education of head:	
Less than 8 years	79
8 years	72
9-11 years	64
12 years	53
13-15 years	54
16 years or more	40
Type of family:	
Husband-wife	68
Wife in paid labor force	48
Wife not in paid labor force	73
Other male head	61
Female head	76
Color of head:	
White	67
Nonwhite	76

* Worked 50-52 weeks.

NOTE: Data relate to families and exclude unrelated individuals. Poverty is defined to include all families with total money income of less than $3000; these are also referred to as poor families. Persistence of poverty is measured by the percent[age] of poor families in 1962 that are also poor in 1963.

Data based on sample of families living at same address as year earlier; movers, whose characteristics could differ from nonmovers, are excluded. In addition, implied changes based on two interviews a year apart for the same family are particularly affected by response errors.

Data are not entirely comparable to those shown in Table 2. See note to that Table.
Source: U.S. Department of Commerce.

simply remain poor. Of the 9.3 million poor families in 1962, 0.6 million were dissolved in 1963, and another 1.8 million—only 19 per cent of the total—moved to a higher income status. Meanwhile 6.9 million remained poor (Table 2) and 1.7 million other families fell into the low-income group.

TABLE 2.

Changes in poverty, 1962-63

Poverty status of family	Estimated number of poor families (millions)
Poor families in 1962	9.3
Less: Families no longer poor in 1963	1.8
Poor families dissolved in 1963	.6
Equals: Families poor in 1962 and 1963	6.9
Plus: Families who became poor in 1963	1.7
Newly formed poor families in 1963	.4
Equals: Poor families in 1963*	9.0

* Families with total money income of less than $3000 (1962 prices).
NOTE: Data relate to families and exclude unrelated individuals. Poor families are defined as all families with total money income of less than $3000.
This table is based on total number of poor families that moved or were dissolved. The persistence rate—74 per cent—derived from this table is somewhat higher than that in Table 1.
Source: CEA.

Of those families leaving poverty in 1963, slightly over two fifths secured incomes between $3000 and $4000, one fifth moved into the $4000-$5000 range, and the remaining two fifths reached or surpassed $5000. Those families whose incomes rose from less than $3000 to $5000 or more undoubtedly included a large number of families where breadwinners returned to full-time work or a new earner found a job. On the other hand, many of those who rose from poverty status, particularly those in the $3000-$4000 bracket in 1963, probably did so only temporarily.

The statistics suggesting that about 20 per cent of the poverty-stricken families in any given year are no longer poor in the following year certainly overstate the degree of real improvement in the income position of this group. They fail to reveal the extent to which many of these families hover about the $3000 income line. An increase in income from $2900 to $3100 hardly constitutes an escape from poverty and, further-

more, may be quickly reversed. Therefore, some measure of poverty
covering more than a one-year period is more appropriate and useful in
identifying the incidence of chronic poverty. A poverty criterion based on
a two-year income average of $3000 yields nearly as many low-income
families as is indicated by the one-year measure.

Employment status

The analysis of poverty in last year's Annual Report emphasized the
importance of economic expansion and rising aggregate employment in
reducing the number of poor families. But it also made clear that many
of the poor—because their family heads are not in the labor force—do
not necessarily benefit from general economic prosperity. Data on work
experience in 1963, shown in Table 3, provide further indications of the

TABLE 3.

Distribution of all and poor families, by work experience of family head, 1963

	Percentage distribu tion	
Work experience of head	All families	Poor families
Total	100	100
In labor force during year:		
Employed all year	67	30
Employed part of year:		
Not unemployed	9	14
Unemployed part of year*	11	16
Not in labor force during year	13	39

* Includes small percent[age] not employed at all during year.
NOTE: Data relate to families and exclude unrelated individuals. *Poor families* are
defined as all families with total money income of less than $3000 (1962 prices).
Detail will not necessarily add to totals because of rounding.
Source: U.S. Department of Labor.

relationship between unemployment and poverty.

Some 30 per cent of families with incomes below $3000 were headed
by persons who held jobs (mostly full-time) throughout the year. An
additional 14 per cent were headed by persons in the labor force during
only part of the year but who were never counted as unemployed because they moved into or out of the labor force. The heads of 16 per cent
of poor families experienced unemployment during 1963. The incidence
of poverty was particularly high among those unemployed for long pe-

riods. A more prosperous economy and stronger job markets would have aided the incomes of all these groups, but particularly the last.

The largest group of poor families—39 per cent of the total—was headed by persons completely out of the labor force during 1963. A few of these family heads, of course, are among "the hidden unemployed"— those employable workers who had withdrawn from or failed to enter the labor force because of discouragement about job opportunities. However, many more of them were retired, disabled, or were women with child-rearing responsibilities.

THE ATTACK ON POVERTY

Passage of the Economic Opportunity Act of 1964 marked the opening of an enlarged attack on inadequate incomes in an economy of relative abundance. The main thrust of this effort is directed at the roots of poverty—particularly at helping the children of the poor. The programs of the Office of Economic Opportunity will provide a community-wide focus for antipoverty efforts by offering education, training, and work experience to help young people escape from poverty. They augment other government programs for education, training, health, and welfare services which deal less specifically with poverty.

REPORT ON THE JANUARY 1964
ECONOMIC REPORT OF THE PRESIDENT

Joint Economic Committee, United States Congress

Each year the JEC presents its views about the Economic Report which the President submits to the Congress. In the first of the following two sections from the JEC statement of 1964, the Democratic majority finds little fault with the call by President Johnson for a war on poverty. However, in the second section, the Republican minority objects strongly to the $3000 poverty line and, thus, to the data presented on the number of poor people. More noteworthy than any disagreements, though, is the fundamental consensus that poverty is not only a serious problem but that its solution requires increased governmental action.

MAJORITY REPORT

The President's proposal for a coordinated and consistent campaign to wage a war on poverty is most welcome. This problem has been neglected too much in past years.

Many forms of poverty have been by one means or another eliminated or their incidence sharply reduced in past decades. Poverty has been reduced from one third to one fifth of the nation's families. Past studies of this committee have listed many federal, state, and local government programs that operate directly or indirectly upon the problems of low-income families. A subcommittee report also recommended several score changes in programs for dealing with the problems of the low-income population living at substandard levels.[1]

In recommending that the Congress cooperate with the President's suggestions, we wish to emphasize the importance of coordination and improved efficiency in their implementation. [If we] consider . . . the extent of past efforts, the fact that there is still a large problem of low-

From the *Report on the January 1964 Economic Report of the President*, Joint Economic Committee, 1964.

income families suggests that the administration of programs already authorized has fallen short of appropriate standards. We concur particularly with the President's judgment that it would be folly to view any program for dealing with low incomes as promising quick or easy results.

In connection with the program, we recommend that our colleagues in Congress, as well as the Administration, keep in mind two basic propositions: (1) expenditures to improve the status of low-income families in many cases must result in raising their productivity, now far below the national average; therefore, such programs may, in a sense, be self-financing by producing a rise in national output far greater than any other investment of similar size and duration; (2) the other large category of low-income families, consisting of those who are aged or suffering from mental or physical illnesses or disabilities, can be helped only by improved public and private provision insurance against the difficulties of their condition.

We suggest that in its early stages the development of a successful pattern of coordinated attacks on the causes of low income and its associated evils will require the operation of several types of projects which will give, at the same time, a practical demonstration of what can be done with a coordinated attack in each selected area while providing the experimental opportunities necessary to sharpen existing tools.

The hope and expectation of results from the proposed war on poverty will be greatly enhanced, we believe, by the general support given it by the minority members of this committee in their separate views. The program which they propose, we are gratified to note, finds much basis in the earlier studies and reports of this committee.

MINORITY REPORT

The War on Poverty

No one can travel through our nation's major urban centers, its small towns or its rural areas without becoming acutely and painfully aware that too many of our citizens of all races, creeds, and colors live outside the mainstream of American society. Many of these individuals have an inadequate opportunity to develop their full potential as human beings and citizens. The greatest domestic challenge before the nation is to accentuate and extend the vast successes of our system in order to realize the promise of the free and open society for all our people. We shall continue to support the assault on poverty as a major step toward this goal.

A war on poverty will not be won by slogans; nor by shopworn programs dressed up in new packaging; nor by the defeatist relief concept of the 1930s; nor by the cynical use of poverty for partisan political ends; nor by overstating the problem and thereby inexcusably lowering America's prestige in the eyes of the world.

The war on poverty will cruelly deceive the poor and their children unless it is new in concept and embraces programs which hit at the root causes of poverty rather than its symptoms. Programs designed to relieve symptoms may produce quick and apparent results. But if our limited physical and intellectual resources are devoted primarily to attacking symptoms, rather than root causes, the war on poverty will turn into a hopelessly inadequate salvage operation that will be judged as having done too little, too late.

Our approach to the problem, which will be outlined in more detail in the recommendations section of this statement, emphasizes programs to prevent the rise of more poverty and to help the existing poor break out of the vicious cycle of poverty in which they find themselves.

There are two preconditions to the success of specific and selective antipoverty measures. One is balanced and sustained economic growth without inflation. The other requirement is vigorous civil rights enforcement to guarantee equal job and educational opportunities for our minorities.

It is also important not to sweep the unemployed under the welfare rug. The unemployed person wants a job, not a caseworker.

The Administration has ignored the seriousness of the continued increase in the cost of living and the steady erosion of the purchasing power of our people—especially of those living on Social Security, pensions, and insurance. Millions of our citizens will not receive a tax reduction from the multibillion-dollar tax bill because they do not have enough income to pay an income tax. But they will suffer from the inflation that will accompany the Administration's fiscal policies. There is no more certain way of worsening poverty in America than by permitting a continuation and acceleration of the postwar inflation.

Aside from the general comments above, we believe that specific antipoverty actions should include, but not necessarily be limited to: (a) developing each program—including those concerned with regional development—to insure that the benefits will accrue directly to families and individuals living in poverty; (b) providing solutions to the problems of low-income families growing out of programs, such as urban renewal and public housing, which were originally designed to assist them; (c) improving rehabilitation programs for the physically handicapped; (d) lifting children out of a poverty environment by federally assisted programs, including residence schools for certain disadvantaged children; (e) increasing the numbers of professionally trained public and private welfare and social workers; (f) upgrading schools in "poverty-impacted" neighborhoods; and (g) conducting research on the relationship between population control and the reduction of poverty.

We also wish to call attention to the initiative and imagination of President Eisenhower and his Council of Economic Advisers in coming to grips with the problem of poverty in America. In 1956, the President's *Economic Report,* particularly Chapter 3, discussed "the extension of prosperity to the less flourishing sectors of the economy" in detail, with particular emphasis on the pockets of chronic unemployment, low-income families in rural areas, vocational rehabilitation, and the need for a more general program of insurance against catastrophic illness. President Eisenhower's 1956 *Report* is a valuable tool for understanding the causes and cures of poverty in America. The late President Kennedy also called attention to these problems.

HOW MANY ARE POOR?

Before proceeding to discuss our own policy proposals, we wish to examine the standards by which poverty is measured and the progress that has been made in reducing poverty in the past decade.

All estimates of the extent of poverty of the kind presented in the 1964 *Economic Report* of the President have a systematic upward bias which paints conditions worse than they are. For example, in most cases a family with insufficient income for a year or less will not be reduced to poverty. Usually a family is not poor in the accepted sense if in the first year of its existence as a family it earns a small income on an annual basis; families are formed in December as well as in January. An independent businessman is not poor just because he earns practically no net income during a year or two while he is establishing his business. A graduate student and his family are not poor within the meaning relevant to the present context. A family with a fluctuating income—high in one year, low in another—is not poor in each year in which its income is low. And some of the well-to-do may live on their accumulated wealth rather than on income for a number of years, while retired persons may live comfortably on the savings they have set aside for just that purpose.

A given money income provides for widely differing levels of living. The Administration says that a family lives in poverty if it has a cash income of under $3000. But families differ substantially in size, age, and living costs. Regional living costs vary substantially and may be twice as great in dollar terms in a Northern city as on a Southern farm.

The Administration's definition of poverty also excludes a family's assets. A family with 600 shares of IBM stock would have had an income of $3000 in 1963, but the shares were worth more than $300,000. In 1962, the Survey of Consumer Finances found that over half of the aged with incomes below $3000 had liquid assets of $1000 or more and that 18 per cent had liquid assets of $5000 or more. Moreover, income in kind is excluded, although this is important for many families, particularly in rural areas.

The Office of Business Economics of the U.S. Department of Commerce confirms the generally accepted and sensible view that noncash income, such as the net-rent o[n] owner-occupied dwellings and home-produced food and fuel, should be included in a family's total income. By this more reasonable definition, 13.6 per cent of the U.S. families—not 20 per cent—had incomes under $3000 in 1961. Although not yet available, the figures for 1962 and 1963 will almost certainly be lower. Another measure of poverty is provided by a census study showing that one in eight—rather than one in five—Americans is poor, based upon ability to qualify for assistance under the welfare laws of the state where they live.

In the February issue of the Morgan Guaranty Survey, it is pointed out that fault can be found with the selection by the CEA, for yardstick purposes, of the [U.S.] Census Bureau's household survey data. For the most part these are based on memory rather than records. They also are characterized by a substantial underreporting of income.

When the sample data for 1962 are blown up to full population size, they yield a money income of $352 billion, or $53 billion *less* than that calculated by the [U.S.] Department of Commerce on the basis of consolidated income tax returns. The Commerce Department's estimate is $68 billion higher (roughly equivalent to total personal income in the United Kingdom) if total nonmoney income also is included.

A study by the University of Michigan Survey Research Center found that 40 per cent of those families with incomes of less than $3000 in 1960 owned cars. About 45 per cent of the families in the $2000-$3000 income range owned their own homes in 1962, as did 42 per cent in the $1000-$2000 income bracket and 35 per cent in the less than $1000 bracket. Of those homeowners with incomes between $2000 and $3000, 66 per cent had no mortgage on their homes. The *Economic Report* notes parenthetically that about 40 per cent of all poor families have some equity in a house.

Herman P. Miller, a special assistant in the U.S. Census Bureau, pointed out recently that "when we probe a little deeper" into living conditions in the severely depressed areas of Harlan County, Ky., it is found that 88 per cent of the homes have washing machines, 67 per cent have a television, 45 per cent have a telephone, and 59 per cent have a car.

No objective definition of poverty exists. The definition varies from place to place and time to time. In America as our standard of living rises, so does our idea of what is substandard. Although too many Americans remain poor, most of them are better off than the poor of earlier years and far better off than the poor in other countries around the world.

HOW FAR HAVE WE COME?

As we look ahead to the task before us, we should be aware of how far America has come in conquering poverty. Since 1947, the proportion of all families with low incomes (in constant 1962 prices) has declined from 32 to 20 per cent in 1962. The principal reason for this progress has been rapid economic growth. Also contributing to reducing poverty has been the development of Social Security, private pension and deferred profit-sharing plans, unemployment compensation, hospitalization, and other forms of insurance. Favorable developments have been offset to some degree by population trends, principally the faster-than-average increase in the population over sixty-five and the increasing desire of the aged to maintain separate households.

The total public and private effort to reduce poverty and human suffering has resulted in an increase of 78 per cent in constant (fiscal 1963) dollar per capita annual expenditures for health, education, and welfare from 1953 to 1963. During the same ten-year period, the share of the total output of the U.S. economy devoted to health, education, social insurance, and welfare has risen from nearly 12 per cent of the gross national product to nearly 18 per cent. This is a particularly impressive performance in the light of other heavy drafts on the economy for defense, space exploration, new highways, urban renewal, and higher consumption.

The percentage of persons in paid employment covered or eligible for coverage under the old-age, survivors', and disability insurance program rose from 80 to 90 per cent between the end of 1952 and the end of

1962. At the end of 1962, 78 per cent of the population over sixty-five were eligible and 71 per cent were receiving benefits under the program. Total monthly OASDI benefits rose from $205 million in December 1952 to nearly $1.2 billion in December 1962.

Private pensions increased more than threefold from $600 million to $2.2 billion between 1953 and 1963—and they are certain to grow considerably in the years ahead. Private pensioners and their wives now total about 15 per cent of the aged population. These private pensions largely supplement benefits of all public programs under which 80 per cent of all aged persons in mid-1962 were getting a regular income. About 84 per cent of all poor families were covered by Social Security or other governmental pensions in 1959.

Vendor medical payments under public assistance increased nearly sevenfold from $154 million to $1 billion during the 1953-63 period. Annual cash benefits under private employee benefit plans tripled from $1.5 to $4.5 billion. Medical benefits under private insurance quadrupled from $1.8 to $7 billion annually, with about three fourths of private medical insurance being provided through private employee benefit plans.

Private philanthropy for institutional care, family counseling, recreation and day-care services, and emergency relief rose to $1.3 billion in 1963 from $785 million ten years earlier. All private charitable contributions now exceed $8.5 billion per year.

During the 1953-63 period, expenditures on medical research increased from $88 million annually to $938 million, while expenditures for maternal and child health and for crippled children's services rose sharply, as did expenditures for vocational rehabilitation programs.

NEW APPROACH NEEDED

To point out the vast amount that has been done to reduce poverty is not to say that the job is finished. It is ironic that many of our welfare programs, such as unemployment insurance, help the poor least of all. Even Social Security is not primarily for the very poor. The breadwinner of a retired couple would have to earn an income considerably above the Administration's $3000 poverty line most of his life in order to get the maximum Social Security payment.

The farm situation also is illustrative. Under this Administration's policies, there has been an increase in the cost-price squeeze of farmers and a decline in the farm sector's share in the national net income. In turn, millions of small farmers, tenant farmers, and farmworkers and their families have been thrust into the poverty sector.

Similarly slum-clearance programs primarily have benefited the middle third of the nation while many of those made homeless by these programs often have been pressed into other slum areas or areas about to become slums.

Greater concentration and attention must be devoted to solving problems of our low-income citizens caused by programs which originally were designed to assist them. House Republicans have already taken the initiative in the area of housing by introducing a comprehensive housing bill directed to perfecting urban renewal and public housing projects on behalf of low-income citizens.

The fact that the poor are out of the direct reach of many federal welfare-type programs means that a wholly new approach is needed. One of the most difficult problems in finding new approaches is that they should help to cure poverty and mitigate its penalties without undermining incentives to effort and success.

One fact is clear. In the American system, the federal government's role in the war on poverty will be far less than that which will be played at the state, local, and neighborhood level, particularly by business, organized labor, and nonprofit enterprises.

The primary reason for local and selective approaches is that persons living in poverty are not a homogeneous group. Nearly all have one or more "handicapping" characteristics but differ in others. The racial-minority family, the family with a female head, or with a head over sixty-five years of age, the family with no earner, or with a head not in the labor force—these are particularly susceptible to poverty, although granted that many of these families are in average or better-than-average circumstances. One unifying characteristic, aside from prolonged illness or physical handicaps, is the coincidence of poverty and little education.

One area of decisive importance for federal government action is civil rights. Poverty arising from the denial of adequate job and educational opportunities to members of minority groups is a blight on the nation, the removal of which can be greatly hastened by vigorous federal leadership.

The policies which the Administration has thus far proposed to combat poverty are inadequate to the task. Not a single policy is directed specifically at poor families. Instead, they are directed at all families. In some cases, such as improving regional economies, it is likely that as much as 80 per cent of the benefits would accrue to nonpoor families. Each policy recommended by the Administration to deal with poverty should be examined to see what share of the benefits will accrue to families with cash and noncash incomes under $3000.

Effective work in attacking poverty is being done by welfare agencies, both private and public, at the local level. Much of this work is assisted by federal funds. We must not permit federal programs to draw off from the local level trained personnel that are in tragically short supply. Local welfare workers already are underpaid and overworked. They are on the frontlines of the war on poverty. That war will not be won soon, but progress requires that the ranks of professionally trained welfare and social workers be increased and the quality of training improved. We recommend that immediate attention be given to developing a combined federal-state-local matching grant program to work toward these objectives.

CHILDREN OF THE POOR

It is only realistic to recognize that in some cases it will be difficult to lift adults out of a poverty status. Rehabilitation can do much for the physically handicapped, and such programs should be broadened and improved. However, lack of basic education, inadequate motivation, health or mental deficiencies, handicapping habits (such as alcoholism), as well as other factors often will militate against a successful effort.

This tragic condition points to the special importance which should be attached to helping the children of the poor. It is they who have the best chance of escaping poverty. A child lifted out of poverty breaks the vicious cycle by which poverty can be passed on to the next generation.

For some children the best hope of lifting them out of poverty is to remove them from a poverty environment which may dull or deaden motivation, incentives and learning. Often this environment is in the slum centers of our major cities.

We recommend that consideration be given to setting up a pilot program on a federal-state matching-grant basis which would work toward this objective. Carefully selected underprivileged children would live and study at public expense at special residence schools operated by states outside the slum area. Admission should be strictly voluntary. The program should be developed and operated in such a manner as to draw on the knowledge and experience of private educational, charitable, business, and labor groups to the maximum extent possible.

The cost of such a program would be small compared to the $4.3 billion in payments to public-assistance recipients in 1963. To this figure, which is about 15 per cent of the nation's total public and private education bill, should be added the other staggering social costs of poverty. Such a program—if successful—would richly reward us all in terms of children equipped to build a future for themselves and to make a constructive contribution to society.

Why is it that schools in poverty neighborhoods so often deteriorate? Shouldn't schools for disadvantaged children be among the best? Who needs good schools more than the children of the poor? A clean, attractive, well-equipped, and well-staffed school in a deteriorating neighborhood could serve as an example and an inspiration for many of our disadvantaged children. We urge that public and private educational groups direct their attention to upgrading the quality of schools in poverty neighborhoods. The federal government now provides special financial assistance to schools in so-called federally impacted areas. We urge that a similar approach be considered for "poverty-impacted" neighborhoods.

No discussion of poverty would be complete without a comment on the impact of population control on the reduction of poverty both at home and abroad. A relationship exists between the population explosion and the conditions existing in many of the underdeveloped nations. Education and research hold out real hope for solutions to this problem.

In this connection, we call attention to the fact that in our own country nearly 4 million persons now receive relief under the aid-to-dependent-children program—a rise of 78 per cent since 1955. A tragically increasing number of these are unwed mothers whose children frequently go on the relief rolls once they reach the required age. This is only one manifestation of the population control problem, but its increasing incidence in the United States calls for action.

The most underdeveloped resource in America is the poor. Recognizing this, America has been conducting a war on poverty since its foundation. More progress in reducing poverty has been made within the framework of the people's capitalism of the United States than anywhere else in the world.

The challenge which still remains is twofold: (1) to provide the poor with job opportunities in an environment of balanced and sustained economic growth without inflation, and (2) to raise the productivity of the poor who already have jobs. Meeting this challenge will realize the promise of our free and open society for all citizens.

NOTES

1. "Low-Income Families and Economic Stability," S. Doc. 146, 81st Cong., 2d sess.; "A Program for the Low-Income Population at Substandard Levels of Living," S. Rept. 1311, 84th Cong., 2d sess.; "Selected Government Programs Which Aid the Unemployed and Low-Income Families," Joint Committee Print, 81st Cong., 1st sess.; and "The Low-Income Population and Economic Growth," Joint Committee Print, 86th Cong., 1st sess.

POVERTY: THE SPECIAL CASE OF THE NEGRO

Alan Batchelder

The economic plight of low-income people is not always portrayed adequately by conventional statistics. In this section of his article, which was presented at the annual meeting of the American Economic Association in December 1964, Alan B. Batchelder argues that poverty and unemployment handicaps of Negroes are more severe than data on income and educational attainments suggest. He discusses, for example, some effects of discrimination on the prices Negro consumers must pay and on the quality of education their children receive. Batchelder is Associate Professor of Economics at Kenyon College. His research has included studies on the changing economic position of Negroes, and on recent programs to retrain the unemployed.

FIRST, SOME HISTORICAL PERSPECTIVE

When considering American Negro affairs, one must remember that [the] social and economic conditions of Negroes are most responsive to changes in unemployment rates. In 1900, 90 per cent of American Negroes lived in the South, most [of them] on farms. The few urban Negroes were totally excluded from manufacturing and from all but menial and laborious jobs. The situation changed to the Negro's advantage only during . . . [the two world] wars. Wartime labor shortages induced managers of large manufacturing corporations to admit Negroes to the production jobs that permitted Negroes to make relative income gains.

During peacetime, the Negro position remained the same or deteriorated. When labor markets "softened" between 1949 and 1959, the income position of Negro men relative to that of white men fell in every section of the country. Rising productivity cut the number of whites and

From "Poverty: The Special Case of the Negro," by Alan Batchelder, *American Economic Review, Papers and Proceedings* (May 1965). Excerpted and reprinted by permission of the American Economic Association and Alan Batchelder.

Negroes living in poverty, but the incidence of poverty among Negroes rose between 1950 and 1962 from two to two and one-half times the white rate.

The past decade's many admonitions and laws opposing discrimination could not, by themselves, raise the Negro's relative economic position in the face of rising unemployment. If Negroes are to approach economic and civil equality in the future, unemployment rates must fall. . . .

THE NEGRO DOLLAR: SECOND-CLASS MONEY

When . . . statistics of poverty [are cited] the portion of Negro families receiving incomes below a particular figure—e.g., $3000—is often compared with the portion of white families receiving incomes below . . . [that figure]. Such comparisons implicitly assume the Negro's $3000 buys as much as the white[man's] $3000.

It does not.

American cities have two housing markets: the citywide white market and the circumscribed Negro market. Because supply is restricted, Negroes "receive less housing value for their dollars spent than do whites. . . . Census statistics indicate that . . . nonwhite renters and homeowners obtain fewer standard-quality dwellings and frequently less space than do whites paying the same amounts." A Chicago welfare department study found "housing defects significantly greater for Negro than for white families, despite the fact that rents for Negro families are 28 per cent a month higher than for whites in private dwellings."

Landlords are sometimes judged greedy extortionists for charging Negro tenants higher rents than whites. But they are operating in a market of restricted supply; high Negro rents reflect supply-and-demand relationships, not conspiratorial landlord greed. . . . [Nevertheless, because] 15 per cent of the consumption expenditures of urban Negro families is for shelter, [their] real income is significantly reduced by relatively high rents.

Poor urban Negroes also pay more than whites for identical consumer durables bought on credit. (Negroes pay more than whites for residential financing too.) The difference may . . . [arise from the] white[s'] reluctance to sell to Negroes, . . . [from] Negro immobility, or . . . [from] the sellers' assumption that poor Negroes are poorer risks than poor whites. Whatever the cause, real income suffers.

Poor Negro families average a half-person larger than poor white families. Consequently, per capita real income of poor Negroes is even farther below [the] per capita real income of poor whites with the same money income.

If, then, $3000 in Negro money buys only as much as $2800 or even $2500 in white money and is distributed over more people, one should keep in mind appropriate reservations when comparing percentage of whites with percentage of Negroes below some income level. . . .

EDUCATION: THE ILLITERATE FALL FARTHER BEHIND

Improved education is manifested in [the] rising median [number of] school years completed. In 1950, Negro medians for men and for women, past age twenty-four, lagged white medians by 2.8 years. By 1960, Negro medians had pushed up a year and a third. So had white medians. Average Negroes remained in the same relative position, but rising educational medians increased the comparative disadvantage of the 2.265 million nonwhite functional illiterates (less than five years of school) making up 23.5 per cent of the 1960 nonwhite population past age twenty-four.

Many poor whites are illiterate, but figures on [the number of] school years completed understate the number of illiterate Negroes and the size of their educational disadvantage. Understatements result for Negroes because so many attended inefficient, segregated Southern schools. Testing poor Negro literacy, Illinois departments of public aid recently sampled able-bodied Negroes aged sixteen to sixty-four receiving public assistance (*not* a random sample of all Negroes). Each person was asked his school attainment; each took the *New Stanford Reading Test*. Of persons educated in Illinois, 3 per cent were functionally illiterate; 35 per cent tested as illiterate. Of persons educated in Mississippi, 23 per cent were functionally illiterate; 81 per cent—four [out] of [every] five adults—tested as illiterate.

Of nonwhites living [in the] North or West in 1960, 41 per cent had been born in the South. These educationally deprived poor Southern Negroes are increasingly disadvantaged in regions where the median education of the local labor force and the quality of local schools rise each year.

Poor Negro boys are specially disadvantaged because of parental limitations and because their homes and the larger society offer so few successful men inspiring academic emulation. Special counseling and educational arrangements can offset those conditions and send slum boys to college, but society devotes few resources to such arrangements.

Left ever farther behind rising national educational norms, poor Negro families are ever less qualified to compete for jobs or to help their children acquire the education required to escape poverty. . . . [Improvement of] education benefits the general public but injures poor Negroes moving from the South to the North and West. . . .

TRANSFER PAYMENTS: PATERNAL SUBSTITUTE AND GOLDEN AGE EQUALIZER

[Another] difference between poor Negroes and poor whites is in the effects of transfer payments. For fifteen years, Negro unemployment rates have been double white rates. This distinguishes Negro from white need for transfers, but does not distinguish poor Negroes from poor whites. . . . [Insofar as] government transfers [are concerned], poor Negroes do differ from poor whites because proportionately more Negro households have feminine heads and proportionately fewer Negroes are past sixty-four.

Relatively few Negroes receive OASDI (old-age, survivors', and disability insurance). In 1962, 6.7 per cent of the 12.5 million recipients were nonwhite. This low figure was . . . [the result of] the nonwhite's shorter age span and the dissimilar work histories that led 73 per cent of elderly whites but only 58 per cent of elderly nonwhites to qualify. In contrast, old-age assistance goes to 38 per cent of elderly nonwhites, [and only] 12 per cent of elderly whites.

OASDI brings elderly Negroes and whites close to income equality. For all persons, Negro income averages half of white income. Yet the average income of nonwhites runs 80 per cent the average total income of whites receiving OASDI. This happens because many Negroes continue in poverty while many whites sink into poverty after retiring.

Because Negro fathers so often decamp, Negro children receive a disproportionate share of ADC (aid to families with dependent children). Of 900,000 families (with 2.8 million children) receiving ADC in 1963, 44 per cent were Negro.

Per capita, ADC pays much less than retirement programs. Old-age assistance meets 94 per cent of the needs of the elderly; ADC supplies 58 per cent of children's needs. Playing surrogate to absent fathers of poor Negro families, ADC never raises incomes or aspirations above levels at which the mothers' and absent fathers' "only legacy to their children is the same one of poverty and deprivation that they received from their own parents." . . .

PERORATION

Because of discrimination in education and employment, there is one last important difference between the Negro and white poor. Logic, rather than statistics, suggests its existence and its implications. To begin, assume the innate ability distribution of Negroes is identical with that of whites. Next, assume the inexorable winnowing out of those least able to earn is the dominant cause of white poverty, but is only a partial cause of Negro poverty. It follows that poor whites are the least able whites, but that poor Negroes include those least able as well as many of middling to superior ability. These able Negroes are poor because of racial discrimination; society denied them access to the channels in which their earning ability could be developed and used.

The economist then concludes that the marginal efficiency of social capital invested in educating and finding work for the Negro poor could be much higher than the marginal efficiency of social capital similarly invested in the white poor. However, we know that the conversion of the poor Negro's potential into dollar product is very difficult in American society. The potential return is latent in the Negro poor. Because Southern segregated Negro schools have placed poor Negroes at a greater disadvantage than poor whites, because racial discrimination keeps qualified Negroes from demanding jobs, because weak labor markets remove the inducement that historically has been most important in helping Negroes score economic gains, it follows that improved education, reduced discrimination or a 3 per cent unemployment level would bring the Negro poor nearer the realization of their latent potential.

PART II

Solutions and Their Prospects

Some Facets of the Administration Program:
Problems and Progress

PRESIDENT JOHNSON'S MESSAGE ON POVERTY, AND THE ECONOMIC OPPORTUNITY ACT OF 1964, A SUMMARY

On March 16, 1964, President Johnson presented to the Congress his first request for antipoverty legislation: the Economic Opportunity Act of 1964. With it, the President submitted this message, in which he urged a national commitment to end poverty, and he outlined broadly the numerous facets of his over-all antipoverty program. A summary of the provisions of the Economic Opportunity Act follows the Presidential message.

PRESIDENT JOHNSON'S MESSAGE ON POVERTY

To the Congress of the United States:

We are citizens of the richest and most fortunate nation in the history of the world.

One hundred and eighty years ago we were a small country struggling for survival on the margin of a hostile land.

Today we have established a civilization of free men which spans an entire continent.

With the growth of our country has come opportunity for our people —opportunity to educate our children, to use our energies in productive work, to increase our leisure—opportunity for almost every American to hope that through work and talent he could create a better life for himself and his family.

The path forward has not been an easy one.

But we have never lost sight of our goal—an America in which every citizen shares all the opportunities of his society, in which every man has a chance to advance his welfare to the limit of his capacities.

We have come a long way toward this goal.

We still have a long way to go.

The distance which remains is the measure of the great unfinished work of our society.

To finish that work I have called for a national war on poverty. Our objective: total victory.

There are millions of Americans—one fifth of our people—who have not shared in the abundance which has been granted to most of us, and on whom the gates of opportunity have been closed.

What does this poverty mean to those who endure it?

It means a daily struggle to secure the necessities for even a meager existence. It means that the abundance, the comforts, the opportunities they see all around them are beyond their grasp.

Worst of all, it means hopelessness for the young.

The young man or woman who grows up without a decent education, in a broken home, in a hostile and squalid environment, in ill health, or in the face of racial injustice—that young man or woman is often trapped in a life of poverty.

He does not have the skills demanded by a complex society. He does not know how to acquire those skills. He faces a mounting sense of despair which drains initiative and ambition and energy.

Our tax cut will create millions of new jobs—new exits from poverty.

But we must also strike down all the barriers which keep many from using those exits.

The war on poverty is not a struggle simply to support people, to make them dependent on the generosity of others.

It is a struggle to give people a chance.

It is an effort to allow them to develop and use their capacities, as we have been allowed to develop and use ours, so that they can share, as others share, in the promise of this nation.

We do this, first of all, because it is right that we should.

From the establishment of public education and land-grant colleges through agricultural extension and encouragement to industry, we have pursued the goal of a nation with full and increasing opportunities for all its citizens.

The war on poverty is a further step in that pursuit.

We do it also because helping some will increase the prosperity of all.

Our fight against poverty will be an investment in the most valuable of our resources—the skills and strength of our people.

And in the future, as in the past, this investment will return its cost many fold to our entire economy.

If we can raise the annual earnings of 10 million among the poor by only $1000 we will have added $14 billion a year to our national output. In addition, we can make important reductions in public-assistance payments which now cost us $4 billion a year, and in the large costs of fighting crime and delinquency, disease and hunger.

This is only part of the story.

Our history has proved that each time we broaden the base of abundance, giving more people the chance to produce and consume, we create new industry, higher production, increased earnings, and better income for all.

Giving new opportunity to those who have little will enrich the lives of all the rest.

Because it is right, because it is wise, and because—for the first time in our history—it is possible to conquer poverty, I submit, for the consideration of the Congress and the country, the Economic Opportunity Act of 1964.

The Act does not merely expand old programs or improve what is already being done.

It charts a new course.

It strikes at the causes, not just the consequences of poverty.

It can be a milestone in our 180-year search for a better life for our people.

This act provides five basic opportunities:

· It will give almost half a million underprivileged young Americans the opportunity to develop skills, continue education, and find useful work.

· It will give every American community the opportunity to develop a comprehensive plan to fight its own poverty—and help them to carry out their plans.

· It will give dedicated Americans the opportunity to enlist as volunteers in the war against poverty.

· It will give many workers and farmers the opportunity to break through particular barriers which bar their escape from poverty.

· It will give the entire nation the opportunity for a concerted attack on poverty through the establishment, under my direction, of the Office of Economic Opportunity, a national headquarters for the war against poverty.

This is how we propose to create these opportunities.

First, we will give high priority to helping young Americans who lack skills, who have not completed their education, or who cannot complete it because they are too poor.

The years of high school and college age are the most critical stage of a young person's life. If they are not helped then, many will be condemned to a life of poverty which they, in turn, will pass on to their children.

I therefore recommend the creation of a Job Corps, a work-training program, and a work-study program.

A new national Job Corps will build toward an enlistment of 100,000 young men. They will be drawn from those whose background, health, and education make them least fit for useful work.

Those who volunteer will enter more than one hundred camps and centers around the country.

Half of these young men will work, in the first year, on special conservation projects to give them education, useful work experience, and to enrich the natural resources of the country.

Half of these young men will receive, in the first year, a blend of training, basic education, and work experience in job training centers.

These are not simply camps for the underprivileged. They are new educational institutions, comparable in innovation to the land-grant colleges. Those who enter them will emerge better qualified to play a productive role in American society.

A new national work-training program operated by the Department of Labor will provide work and training for 200,000 American men and women between the ages of sixteen and twenty-one. This will be developed through state and local governments and nonprofit agencies.

Hundreds of thousands of young Americans badly need the experience, the income, and the sense of purpose which useful full or part-time work can bring. For them such work may mean the difference between finishing school or dropping out. Vital community activities from hospitals and playgrounds to libraries and settlement houses are suffering because there are not enough people to staff them.

We are simply bringing these needs together.

A new national work-study program operated by the Department of Health, Education, and Welfare will provide federal funds for part-time jobs for 140,000 young Americans who do not go to college because they cannot afford it.

There is no more senseless waste than the waste of the brainpower and skill of those who are kept from college by economic circumstance. Under this program they will, in a great American tradition, be able to work their way through school.

They and the country will be richer for it.

Second, through a new community-action program we intend to strike at poverty at its source—in the streets of our cities and on the farms of our countryside, among the very young and the impoverished old.

This program asks men and women throughout the country to prepare long-range plans for the attack on poverty in their own local communities.

These are not plans prepared in Washington and imposed upon hundreds of different situations.

They are based on the fact that local citizens best understand their own problems, and know best how to deal with those problems.

These plans will be local plans striking at the many unfilled needs which underlie poverty in each community, not just one or two. Their components and emphasis will differ as needs differ.

These plans will be local plans calling upon all the resources available to the community—federal and state, local and private, human and material.

And when these plans are approved by the Office of Economic Opportunity, the federal government will finance up to 90 per cent of the additional cost for the first two years.

The most enduring strength of our nation is the huge reservoir of talent, initiative, and leadership which exists at every level of our society.

Through the community-action program we call upon this, our greatest strength, to overcome our greatest weakness.

Third, I ask for the authority to recruit and train skilled volunteers for the war against poverty.

Thousands of Americans have volunteered to serve the needs of other lands.

Thousand more want the chance to serve the needs of their own land.

They should have that chance.

Among older people who have retired, as well as among the young, among women as well as men, there are many Americans who are ready to enlist in our war against poverty.

They have skills and dedication. They are badly needed.

If the state requests them, if the community needs and will use them, we will recruit and train them and give them the chance to serve.

Fourth, we intend to create new opportunities for certain hard-hit groups to break out of the pattern of poverty.

Through a new program of loans and guarantees we can provide incentives to those who will employ the unemployed.

Through programs of work and retraining for unemployed fathers and mothers we can help them support their families in dignity while preparing themselves for new work.

Through funds to purchase needed land, organize cooperatives, and create new and adequate family farms we can help those whose life on the land has been a struggle without hope.

Fifth, I do not intend that the war against poverty become a series of uncoordinated and unrelated efforts—that it perish for lack of leadership and direction.

Therefore this bill creates, in the Executive Office of the President, a new Office of Economic Opportunity. Its director will be my personal chief of staff for the war against poverty. I intend to appoint Sargent Shriver to this post.

He will be directly responsible for these new programs. He will work with and through existing agencies of the Government.

This program—the Economic Opportunity Act—is the foundation of our war against poverty. But it does not stand alone.

For the past three years this government has advanced a number of new proposals which strike at important areas of need and distress.

I ask the Congress to extend those which are already in action, and to establish those which have already been proposed.

There are programs to help badly distressed areas such as the Area Redevelopment Act, and the legislation now being prepared to help Appalachia.

There are programs to help those without training find a place in today's complex society—such as the Manpower Development Training Act and the Vocational Education Act for youth.

There are programs to protect those who are specially vulnerable to the ravages of poverty—hospital insurance for the elderly, protection for migrant farm workers, a food-stamp program for the needy, coverage for millions not now protected by a minimum wage, new and expanded unemployment benefits for men out of work, a housing and community-development bill for those seeking decent homes.

Finally there are programs which help the entire country, such as aid to education which, by raising the quality of schooling available to every American child, will give a new chance for knowledge to the children of the poor.

I ask immediate action on all these programs.

What you are being asked to consider is not a simple or an easy program. But poverty is not a simple or an easy enemy.

It cannot be driven from the land by a single attack on a single front.

Were this so we would have conquered poverty long ago.

Nor can it be conquered by government alone.

For decades American labor and American business, private institutions and private individuals have been engaged in strengthening our economy and offering new opportunity to those in need.

We need their help, their support, and their full participation.

Through this program we offer new incentives and new opportunities for cooperation, so that all the energy of our nation, not merely the efforts of government, can be brought to bear on our common enemy.

Today, for the first time in our history, we have the power to strike away the barriers to full participation in our society. Having the power, we have the duty.

The Congress is charged by the Constitution to "provide . . . for the general welfare of the United States." Our present abundance is a measure of its success in fulfilling that duty. Now Congress is being asked to extend that welfare to all our people.

The President of the United States is President of all the people in every section of the country. But this office also holds a special responsibility to the distressed and disinherited, the hungry and the hopeless of this abundant nation.

It is in pursuit of that special responsibility that I submit this message to you today.

The new program I propose is within our means. Its cost of $970 million is 1 per cent of our national budget—and every dollar I am requesting for this program is already included in the budget I sent to Congress in January.

But we cannot measure its importance by its cost.

For it charts an entirely new course of hope for our people.

We are fully aware that this program will not eliminate all the poverty in America in a few months or a few years. Poverty is deeply rooted and its causes are many.

But this program will show the way to new opportunities for millions of our fellow citizens.

It will provide a lever with which we can begin to open the door to our prosperity for those who have been kept outside.

It will also give us the chance to test our weapons, to try our energy and ideas and imagination for the many battles yet to come. As conditions change, and as experience illuminates our difficulties, we will be prepared to modify our strategy.

And this program is much more than a beginning.

Rather, it is a commitment. It is a total commitment by this President, and this Congress, and this nation, to pursue victory over the most ancient of mankind's enemies.

On many historic occasions the President has requested from Congress the authority to move against forces which were endangering the well-being of our country.

This is such an occasion.

On similar occasions in the past we have often been called upon to wage war against foreign enemies which threatened our freedom. Today we are asked to declare war on a domestic enemy which threatens the strength of our nation and the welfare of our people.

If we now move forward against this enemy—if we can bring to the challenges of peace the same determination and strength which has brought us victory in war—then this day and this Congress will have won a secure and honorable place in the history of the nation, and the enduring gratitude of generations of Americans yet to come.

LYNDON B. JOHNSON.

THE WHITE HOUSE, *March 16, 1964.*

A SUMMARY OF THE ECONOMIC OPPORTUNITY ACT OF 1964

Fiscal 1965 Authorization: $974.5 million

The Economic Opportunity Act of 1964 establishes an Office of Economic Opportunity in the Executive Office of the President. The OEO is headed by a director who has a planning and coordinating staff responsible for coordinating the poverty-related programs of all Government agencies. Within the OEO, separate staffs operate a Job Corps, a program for Volunteers In Service To America (VISTA), a Community-Action Program, and special programs for migrant workers. In addition, the OEO distributes funds to existing agencies to operate other programs authorized under the bill: work-training programs administered through the [U.S.] Labor Department; work-study programs and adult basic education through [U.S. Department of] Health, Education, and Welfare; special rural antipoverty programs through [the U.S. Department of] Agriculture; small business loans through the Small Business Administration; and community work and training projects for welfare recipients through [U.S. Department of] Health, Education, and Welfare.

Following is a summary of the programs authorized under the Economic Opportunity Act of 1964:

Title I. Youth Programs: $412.5 million

Part A—Establishes a Job Corps to provide education, work experience, and vocational training in conservation camps and residential training centers; would enroll 40,000 young men and women, aged sixteen to twenty-one, this year, 100,000 next year. Administered by the oeo. Total cost: $190 million.

Part B—Establishes a Work-Training Program under which the director of the oeo enters into agreements with state and local governments or nonprofit organizations to pay part of the cost of full- or part-time employment to enable 200,000 young men and women, sixteen to twenty-one, to continue or resume their education or to increase their employability. Administered by the U.S. Labor Department. Total cost: $150 million.

Part C—Establishes a Work-Study Program under which the director of the oeo enters into agreements with institutions of higher learning to pay part of the costs of part-time employment to permit 140,000 students from low-income families to enter upon or continue higher education. Administered by [the U.S.] Department of Health, Education, and Welfare. Total cost: $72.5 million.

Title II. Community-Action Programs: $340 million

Part A—Authorizes the director of the oeo to pay up to 90 per cent of the costs of antipoverty programs planned and carried out at the community level. Programs will be administered by the communities and will coordinate poverty-related programs of various federal agencies. Total cost: $315 million.

Part B—Authorizes the director of the oeo to make grants to states to provide basic education and literacy training to adults. Administered by the U.S. Department of Health, Education, and Welfare. Total cost: $25 million.

Part C—Authorizes the director of the oeo to establish and operate a clearinghouse to facilitate arrangements between foster parents willing to provide financial support and needy children under the guidance of a local agency. Only administrative funds required.

Title III. Programs to Combat Poverty in Rural Areas: $35 million

Part A—Authorizes loans up to $2500 to very low-income rural families for farm operations and nonagricultural, income-producing enterprises, and loans to low-income family cooperatives. Administered by the U.S. Department of Agriculture.

Part B—Authorizes assistance to establish and operate housing, sanitation, education, and child day-care programs for migrant farm workers and their families. Total cost: not more than $15 million, financed from other Titles.

Part D—Authorizes the Secretary of Agriculture to indemnify farmers whose milk has been polluted by pesticides recommended by the U.S. Department of Agriculture. No specific funds authorized.

Title IV. Employment and Investment Incentives

Authorizes loans and guarantees to small businesses of up to $25,000 on more liberal terms than the regular loan provisions of the Small Business Administration. Administered by the Small Business Administration, [and financed by its] . . . regular spending authority.

Title V. Work-Experience Programs: $150 million

Authorizes the director of the OEO to transfer funds to the U.S. Department of Health, Education, and Welfare to pay costs of experimental, pilot, or demonstration projects designed to stimulate the adoption in the states of programs of providing constructive work experience or training for unemployed fathers and needy persons.

Title VI. Administration and Coordination: $10 million

Establishes the OEO and specifies its functions. Authorizes the director of the OEO to recruit and train an estimated 5000 VISTA volunteers to serve in specified mental health, migrant, Indian, and other federal programs, including the Job Corps, as well as in state and community anti-poverty programs.

Title VII. Treatment of Public Assistance

A policy declaration that an individual's opportunity to participate in programs under this Act shall neither jeopardize, nor be jeopardized by, his receipt of public assistance.

August 20, 1964

STATEMENT ON THE ECONOMIC OPPORTUNITY ACT OF 1964

C. Lowell Harriss

In this statement at the Senate Committee hearings on the Economic Opportunity Act, C. Lowell Harriss raised important questions about the power to be given the program's director, the likelihood of success of the various antipoverty measures, and the relationship between the Act's initial and eventual cost. Note that some of his points involve the effectiveness or efficiency of the Act—whether its benefits will exceed its costs —while others involve equity—whether the program will help those who need it most. Harriss is Professor of Economics at Columbia University, author of The American Economy, *and co-author of* American Public Finance.

Both you and the House Committee on Education and Labor have heard divergent views about means—but probably not about the worth of the objective.*,** Some of you doubtlessly recall the proposals of President Eisenhower, especially those of 1956, for dealing with poverty. A generally prosperous society may overlook the needs of a small minority.

My purpose, certainly, is to contribute in devising effective methods

From the "Prepared Statement on the Economic Opportunity Act," by C. Lowell Harriss, *Hearings on the Economic Opportunity Act,* U.S. Senate Committee on Labor and Public Welfare, 1964.

* The views expressed are my own and not necessarily those of any organization with which I am associated. These comments duplicate to some extent those which I presented to the House Committee on Education and Labor.

** While agreeing that the objective is desirable, reasonable men will differ on the extent, nature, and causes of poverty as well as upon the means most likely to be effective in dealing with it. The importance of this objective in relation to other objectives of public policy will also be subject to debate and difference of judgment. The $3000 figure seems to me needlessly crude because it is meant to apply to "family." Yet size of family differs greatly, as do other conditions. A per capita figure might serve more usefully. Yet brief thought will suggest many difficulties of selecting a figure. No specific amount will be appropriate for all cases.

115

of reducing, and more rapidly, the evils of poverty. . . . The population outlook adds to the need for jobs, especially those which relatively young people can do. One problem of some seriousness deserves far more attention than it receives. Many of the country's biggest employers, certainly the U.S. government, have no jobs at all, or very few, for persons of low skills. If total demand for goods and services were more pressing, these employers would hire persons now considered submarginal and train them on the job—in sufficient numbers to alter the outlook significantly. The opportunities here far exceed those often recognized. More training opportunity at government expense can meet part of the need. Yet I suggest that there must be search for other means of closing the gap between the rising minimum which employers will pay and the "low" productivity of so many job-seekers.*

The majority of us have little contact with the small minority who are truly poor. Who does all that he can to alleviate distress through private philanthropy?

Fortunately, the economic process has worked powerfully and effectively to enlarge opportunity, to raise the lowest incomes. But it does so less rapidly and less completely than desired by men of compassion and goodwill. What would now be involved in enlarging the role of the national government in dealing with poverty?

WHERE TO MOVE NEXT

National government can do some things—and cannot do others. S. 2642 [the Senate number for the Economic Opportunity Bill] involves several new undertakings. Is each something that offers a reasonable prospect of success? Is each better than possible alternatives?

The federal government now has many programs to reduce poverty or its ill effects. Within the last few years it has entered new fields and expanded its efforts in others. Before undertaking new programs, should not the Congress seek more analysis of past and present operations? I do not propose lengthy, study-it-to-death analyses—of area redevelopment, vocational training, aid to small business, nearly thirty years of aid to farmers, aid to dependent children, and so on. Yet Congress and the public do need the results of objective effort to identify (a) accomplishments and disappointments, (b) problems solved and unsolved,

---

* Economic analysis leaves no doubt that an increase in over-all demand resulting from federal budget deficits financed by the creation of money (borrowing from commercial banks which does not curtail capacity for lending to others) can reduce unemployment substantially—but not without upward pressures on the level of prices (inflation).

(c) opportunities for improving the programs to which we are already committed, (d) obstacles to coordination among programs. What is really needed to surmount the difficulties? Where are the people qualified for such tasks? To what extent are present disappointments the result of internal procedures of government? Would new programs be free from conditions which account for some of our present failures—e.g., tens of billions of farm aid over the last fifteen years and yet the persistence of farm poverty—?

How thoroughly have governmental and private agencies "researched" such vital issues as the relative merits of revising and enlarging present programs compared with these new proposals? Have the facts and conclusions of such analyses been made fully available to the Congress? What can you do to obtain such research for aid in evaluating the innovations of the bill before you?

A broad investigation of all that is now being done—a look at the whole, including social insurance—would certainly help in judging how best to proceed.*

Human, organizational, emotional resources are not unlimited. Perhaps, for a time, working to improve present programs would be better than adopting some of the new proposals. How many skilled social workers and administrators are now unemployed? Would not added programs tend to draw personnel from present positions and thereby hamper somewhat the work now being done? My casual impression is that increased demand would "call out" capacity not now evident—but not in adequate quantity; some responsibility would fall upon people not well qualified.

Dreams and aspirations do not always become realities. In proposing to embark on new ventures, one may fail to allow adequately for the limitations of reality—limitations which seem frustrating, even unsurmountable, when trying to improve an existing system. But the alternatives of strengthening present programs do warrant more explicit comparison than, at least to my knowledge, has been supplied to Congress and the public in connection with H.R. 11377 [the House of Representatives number for the Economic Opportunity Bill] and S.2642.

If coal mining is distressed, federal subsidy of nuclear energy seems less than the epitome of wisdom. If a decline in railroad employment causes concern, subsidy of competing means of transport will only aggravate the problem.

---

* Such a study would take considerable time. It should not serve as an excuse for delaying any action which now seems wise. Any new programs, however, should be considered tentative until broad, long-range plans have been made on the basis of thorough analysis of the whole system.

Federal minimum wage legislation may not do much to reduce job opportunities of the young and unskilled. But do we know? . . .

Why not make a determined effort to reduce federal policies whose results included (unintended, undesired, but also undeniable) aggravations of poverty? This committee, I realize, does not have jurisdiction over most of the programs which might be considered in this connection, but I venture three suggestions: (a) More tax reduction. Some taxes fall on the poor. Other taxes impede job creation. The Revenue Acts of 1962 and 1964 have not done all that is reasonably possible over the near future to give tax relief to achieve the objectives of the bill now before you. Enlarging federal expenditures will hardly speed the prospects of more tax relief. (b) Reversal (not precipitous) of policies which raise the price of food—especially when these policies require taxes which to some extent fall on the poor. Does not this possibility deserve a place on the agenda of things the national government does in attacking poverty and its evils? (c) Examination of federal programs to learn which tend to raise living costs or to deprive some men, women, and youths of job opportunities. Any such policies, and their results, are controversial. But do they not warrant attention in debates on an "economic opportunity" program?

What will be the costs? Can we get a clearer picture of the future pricetags for the different elements of the package? The $962 million budgeted for 1965 is not large in the total of over $122 billion federal cash expenditure. One billion dollars may not seem large even in relation to present outlays for federal-state-local programs seeking much the same goals. But what about the future? Which programs would be self-perpetuating and which by their success would work their own extinction?

At least two aspects of cost justify attention. (1) Will the totals grow substantially? If so, we should recognize the implications of what is decided now.* (2) What are likely to be (a) costs per unit and (b) costs in relation to accomplishment? "Costing" of the latter types will be difficult, at times impossible. But the present is the time to face such questions as: How will later evaluations compare costs and accomplishments? What kind of evidence will be sought and used? "Payoffs" may justify an apparently heavy expense; they may not.

How can we judge results in relation to costs—two and five years from now? New departures always involve some risk of partial failure. The

* I am not questioning this country's economic capacity to support big programs to aid the poor, put a man on the moon soon, build highways, and so on. Before adopting new programs, however, we should get the best possible estimates of "ultimate annual cost."

risk is often worth taking if the chances of success are great enough. Where part [of the] results, good and bad, are to significant degree "intangibles," evaluation is inherently so difficult that we can make and perpetuate costly errors. . . . [Although] proper quantification must be hazardous, . . . explicit efforts to relate costs to probable benefits should help in making choices. I do not propose sacrificing humanity to the dollar—but the people who pay the dollars are humans, and some of them may be poorer than some beneficiaries of the program—if not today, perhaps in the future.*

You have been given examples of success—highly impressive examples—in pilot efforts and in programs comparable to those proposed. What has been involved in making for success? Have there been failures? If so, what guidance do they offer? What conditions seem to be associated with differences between success and disappointment? . . .

Unfortunately, application of the tools of economic analysis to many of the proposals seems likely to yield rather little in the way of results which will be concretely helpful. For one thing, vagueness and uncertainty about specifics hamper analysis. For another, much will hinge upon the caliber of administration. And, as just noted, part of the results will consist of intangibles. Divergent conclusions may come from the speculations of equally qualified economists. Nevertheless, more explicit effort to compare benefit and cost now—anticipated and as realized over time—should be helpful in deciding what to do and to what extent.

PROBLEMS OF NATIONAL GOVERNMENT ACTION

Today the national interest in the individual does extend in ways which invite more federal government action than some Americans welcome as a general thing. For example, the possibility of population movement makes us all potential neighbors. The child sitting next to mine in school next year may now live far, far away. National defense demands so much more than before 1940 that everyone has some concern with the capacity of others to contribute—in staffing the Armed Forces, in paying the money costs, in producing what is needed. Consequently, it is argued, individual, business, and state-local effort cannot be counted upon to do all that the interests of others require. In other words, more

* The Federal tax system, though generally progressive, does impose burdens on the poor. No one can identify any particular tax with any particular expenditure. No one, for example, can say with assurance that the dollars for farm aid come from this or that group of taxpayers. Yet we can say with confidence that some parts of the tax system bear upon low-income groups.

than humanitarian reasons exist to persuade all of us to try to speed the reduction of poverty, not only close to home but also throughout the land.

The past extension of federal government activities—types of programs and amounts—proves that the Congress has not overlooked this argument. Before doing more, however, you might well consider the following four points:

1. In a land as varied as ours, one with such huge diversity, action on a nationwide basis is not likely to serve all parts of the country efficiently.* What is excellent for one time, place, or group, will be poor for others and positively bad for some. Rules with national application will represent, or force, many compromises.

S. 2642, of course, includes plans for local initiative and decision. Yet approval by federal officials will often be required. How can men in charge of spending federal funds not feel responsibility for evaluating proposals? In many cases an official's qualifications for judging local projects well must be inherently limited by lack of familiarity with conditions in the specific localities within his jurisdiction. The problem is basic. The issue is not one of goodwill. It is the vastness of the difficulty of adapting national government action to diversity in a way that will assure a reasonable degree of efficiency—i.e., results in relation to costs.

2. The truly poor, fortunately, are a small minority. As a consequence, the really needy, and the teen-agers, do not have many votes. Unfortunately, not all voters can be counted upon to be powerfully motivated for aiding the most unfortunate as were the men and women who prepared the proposals. What can we expect as time passes? Pressures to extend the scope and cost of benefits are likely. Before long, are not at least some of the programs likely to be extended to groups less deserving— the shotgun replacing the rifle? What are the probabilities? And the likely results? The history of area redevelopment may throw light on the practical possibilities of keeping the federal programs pinpointed at greatest need.

3. Would everyone in essentially the same position benefit about equally? At least parts of the program involve rationed benefits—some people getting, others no less deserving being left out—e.g., enrollment in youth programs, gifts to some farmers. Inability to do everything desirable does not argue for inaction. But the Congress, I suggest, should

---

* Space limits prevent me from distinguishing as I should like the elements involved in inherently national problems—defense, monetary policy, antitrust law—and problems which do not necessarily require decisions which apply to the country as a whole.

openly face the implications of government creation of discrimination—among individuals, families, businesses, or areas which are generally similar to each other in the relevant respects. Some of the proposals would use dollars collected from the public as a whole—including the poor—to benefit less than all members of a group with about equally persuasive claims. . . .

4. Mr. Shriver has said: "If, as time goes on, we find that any of our programs is not making a maximum contribution to our total effort, we will change that program or get rid of it—just as large business disposes of those divisions which are unprofitable." But how often does the federal government really act this way? Getting rid of [an] established program can be difficult—especially if the statute must be changed, if a "clientele" of beneficiaries has been built up, or if an administrative organization is functioning. Sweeping modification may be almost as hard to accomplish. Furthermore, how will "maximum contribution" be measured? I am not arguing for inaction. I am urging you to look ahead before you act and try to build in standards for evaluation and provisions for doing what Mr. Shriver recognizes as desirable but which experience suggests can be exceptionally difficult.

These four points, to the extent that they are valid, do not combine to make a case which you should find determining. Yet neither should they be ignored.

POWER OF THE DIRECTOR (HEAD OFFICE)

. . . Mr. Shriver has said that there would be no waste and also that local initiative and decision would play a determining role. Yet if he, his delegates, and successors, are to achieve one of these two goals, how can they be sure of getting the other? What if a dozen or a hundred of the local organizations approve programs (90 or 75 per cent of the cost to be borne by Uncle Sam) which federal officials do not judge to be promising? * On what basis will which official decide to reject a proposal? Or condition approval upon some modification? [Officials are] sometimes limited only by the terms "appropriate" or "necessary." What

* Federal government assumption of such a large portion of the cost of grant-in-aid programs has not been common. Where the sharing of cost has been highly unequal—the interstate highway program—what problems have appeared? How can you get suggestions for preventing trouble in new programs? No one should expect perfection. Yet no one should ignore the possibility that some people who spend money provided by others may be a bit careless.

would these words mean? At point after point the director is authorized —with only the vaguest of limits.

You might well consider giving explicit attention to the definition of several terms of key importance—*low income, long-term unemployed, family farm.* What will *give promise of progress?* What is *maximum feasible participation?* What will *utilize efficiently and expeditiously* mean? Putting definitions into statutes is certain to create one sort of problem. Omitting them creates others. Perhaps the report of the committee would provide an appropriate means of indicating intent without the rigidity which inclusion in the statute would involve. The effort to define would in itself be a helpful exercise.

S. 2642 would enlarge the power of the executive branch of the national government—handing out money here rather than there, for this rather than that, for Mr. A. rather than Mr. B. Would not all members of Congress find themselves subject to added leverage and pressure from the executive branch as the choice of where to dispense federal funds depended upon the discretion of the director? His authority to grant or withhold favors would extend pervasively throughout our economy, society, and political system. Good can come from the use of discretion. The very nature of the program provides appealing reason for seeking a wide range of freedom to adapt. Personally, I can enthuse over the positive potentialities. Yet not all kings are philosophers. The implications of grants of wide discretion should be explored fully.

The influence would run directly from federal officials to local units. Eligible local groups would not necessarily be controlled by the democratic (electoral) process. The enlistment of voluntary, religious, civic, nonpolitical groups in the community-action programs has attractions on more than one score. In some respects this approach has great merit. But the director's power to control funds to finance most of the cost of projects would seem to me the cause of more than minor concern. Let us agree that the goodwill and the competence of present leaders are above question. How many equally qualified persons can they recruit? Moreover, other considerations are vital. We should be seriously concerned about the extension of federal influence into localities and over nonelected organizations. The bill provides so very much leeway—it imposes so few restrictions—that the influence would be both greater and different from that with which we have become familiar in grant-in-aid programs.

CONCLUDING COMMENT

To conclude, I suggest that: (1) In deciding on the next moves careful study be made of present programs and the relative promise of improving them as against setting up new ones; (2) we seek more light on long-run costs and the bases for evaluating results; (3) explicit account be taken of difficulties which are not improbable when the national government undertakes programs like those proposed; (4) for proposals adopted, the grants of power to the director be modified.

POVERTY WAR REPORT

The Wall Street Journal

The translation of an idea into specific action is often troublesome. In this article The Wall Street Journal *describes some of these problems as they arose in the implementation of Neighborhood Youth Corps and Job Corps programs established by the Economic Opportunity Act of 1964. The conflicts that can develop between antipoverty efforts and racial, religious, and labor-union attitudes are illustrated effectively, as are some of the early successes that the antipoverty program produced.*

The opening shots ring out in the Administration's war on poverty. On some fronts the attack rolls smoothly. On others it sputters.

Los Angeles appears to be one of the bright spots; under the Neighborhood Youth Corps program, the schools there are already signing up needy students for part-time jobs that hopefully will keep them from becoming dropouts. The poverty war is also off to a generally auspicious start in Detroit, where impoverished residents have been flocking to four new "community-action" centers offering job training, employment counseling and other services. And in Pittsburgh an official of the committee guiding the poverty program locally says that, as a result of the undertaking, government and welfare agencies that "haven't talked together for years are working together now."

But in Massachusetts the drive against poverty so far has created more rifts than it has healed. One major problem in the Bay State has been organized labor's fears that wages paid under youth employment programs might undercut established pay scales. "We can't see spending one hundred years putting a floor under wages and then having a bunch of social workers blithely tear it down," declares Lawrence C. Sullivan, Executive Secretary of the Boston Labor Council.

From "Poverty War Report," *The Wall Street Journal,* January 18, 1965. Reprinted by permission of *The Wall Street Journal.*

RED TAPE AND RACE

In a number of cities the war on poverty has run into trouble in the form of loud complaints from minority groups—mainly Negroes—that they are not sufficiently represented in the organizations set up to direct the effort. And here and there are heard anguished cries that some aspects of the antipoverty campaign are in danger of becoming hopelessly snarled in red tape.

"If we're going to fill out forms and tell what we did yesterday, all the activities in our office, including poverty, would have to stop," says Raymond Hilliard, Director of the Cook County, Ill[inois], Department of Public Aid and a member of the committee administering the war on poverty in the Chicago area.

Some confusion and friction are obviously to be expected in any venture as broad and varied as the antipoverty drive. Sargent Shriver's Office of Economic Opportunity, which has over-all responsibility for the poverty war, to date has announced some 400 projects involving about $220 million of federal funds.

The detailed planning and execution of the projects are left up to various state, county, and city government agencies as well as private groups. This arrangement, . . . [although] it has the virtue of relying on the judgment of people on the scene instead of putting all decisions in the hands of distant Washington officials, inevitably gives rise to conflicts and problems at the local level as the war on poverty gets under way.

Despite frequent start-up difficulties, however, the antipoverty drive appears to be attracting considerable support around the country.

ATTITUDES IN DETROIT AND DALLAS

"Nobody knows yet whether the war on poverty will succeed or fail," says Edward Connor, Chairman of the Board of Supervisors of Michigan's Wayne County, which includes Detroit. "But the enthusiasm it has generated indicates that people are interested in making a real effort to do something about the problem." Even in such a stronghold of conservatism as Dallas, widespread support has been given to a plan, requiring $300,000 of federal funds, under which the county schools would set up a Neighborhood Youth Corps program.

But would-be poverty fighters sometimes find their zeal diminishes when they try to turn their plans into action. Some impoverished West Virginia communities have had difficulty formulating the detailed anti-poverty plans required by the OEO. Some large cities in other states have had similar troubles, despite their sizable staffs of planners and administrators.

Says Randolph E. Wise, Philadelphia Welfare Commissioner and executive director of the city's antipoverty effort: "Shriver and his people have been critical of our initial programs, yet they offer no concrete solutions. So we don't know exactly what we're supposed to do."

NEW ANTIPOVERTY AGENCIES

In many metropolitan areas new agencies representing a wide range of community interests have been established to oversee the antipoverty campaigns. Thus, New York has set up the Antipoverty Operations Board of New York City, and Detroit has created an organization called Total Action Against Poverty. The Los Angeles area has formed the Economic and Youth Opportunities Agency of Los Angeles County.

But the noble-sounding names leave some citizens unimpressed—particularly those citizens who feel they haven't been given a big enough voice in the poverty organizations. The Greater Cleveland Council for Economic Opportunities, formed last summer, has been hampered from the start by disagreements over representation of civil rights groups and low-income residents. As originally constituted, the Council included no spokesmen for these segments of the community, and there were vociferous objections.

The upshot was a decision to enlarge the Cleveland Council from twenty-two to twenty-five members by adding an official of the National Association for the Advancement of Colored People [NAACP] plus a Negro woman and a white woman from low-income areas. This solution fell far short of the demands of the Council's critics, however, and the situation became further confused when the white woman named to the Council resigned because she didn't want her children to be stigmatized at school as "poor." . . . [Although] the bickering over the makeup of the Cleveland council may not be entirely responsible for the delay, Cleveland has yet to be allocated any federal poverty funds.

Cleveland is not the only area in which civil rights leaders have been critical of poverty programs. In Boston, the NAACP says it will challenge the use of federal funds for the local antipoverty program because a large portion of the money would be handled through the school system, which the NAACP asserts is illegally operating racially imbalanced schools.

The NAACP hasn't said what action it will take, but it says: "If we get the answer we seek on the question of federal funds, the whole anti-poverty campaign will grind to a halt in many cities until the school segregation problem is solved."

In Philadelphia, the Congress of Racial Equality [CORE] has complained of inadequate representation for the poor, many of whom are Negroes, in the management of the city's attack on poverty. Negro leaders in Georgia have been demanding a bigger say in that state's antipoverty efforts. In Louisiana, Negro groups have bitterly protested Gov[ernor] McKeithen's appointment of Shelby Jackson, an ardent segregationist, as the $12,000-a-year assistant director of the state's anti-poverty program. Gov[ernor] McKeithen's answer: "Since most of us in Louisiana believe in segregation, it would be pretty hard to fill that job without appointing a segregationist."

Indians have also become involved in antipoverty controversies. At a recent meeting in Denver, leaders of the National Indian Youth Council, representing tribes from throughout the nation, asked that an Indian be given a high position in the OEO. One council official complained that "Indians have found before, after Congress has voted funds, that very little of the money appropriated gets to the Indian tribe."

On the other hand, a group of whites in the state of Washington is threatening to bring suit to block the establishment of a Job Corps camp, a part of the poverty program which provides board and room for jobless youths and gives them work experience and training, on an Indian reservation at White Swan, Wash[ington]. Although the center would train youths of all races, the complaining citizens say the recreational facilities the Job Corps members would build would benefit only Indians.

But the attorney for the Washington residents fighting the White Swan job camp concedes there are other factors in their opposition. They "don't like the type of persons that might be brought in," he explains.

IMPORTING "DELINQUENTS"?

Similar objections to Job Corps centers have cropped up in a number of other areas. For the most part, they stem from rumors that the establishment of camps locally will result in "delinquents" from all over the country being brought into a community.

This is the case in the small town of Collbran, Colo[rado], where some of the residents are opposing a proposed job camp on the ground it would bring in "undesirable characters." In Lawton, Okla[homa], and

Las Vegas, N[ew] M[exico], many residents have become alarmed about plans to set up job camps because of reports they would be filled with juvenile delinquents from Harlem. . . . [Although] it's true some Job Corps camps may draw youths from a wide area, supporters of the program insist that the camps won't be filled with young toughs and that all Job Corps members will be carefully screened and supervised.

The segment of the antipoverty effort that has drawn union fire is the Neighborhood Youth Corps, which is run by the [U.S.] Labor Department. Besides providing part-time jobs for needy students, this program offers urban youths who have left school a chance to learn marketable skills and gain work experience.

The basic point of dispute is the hourly wage rates to be paid members of the Neighborhood Youth Corps. Many union leaders including AFL-CIO President George Meany have been insisting that pay be at least $1.25 an hour, the federal minimum wage. But some of the officials administering poverty programs locally have sought to pay at lower levels— one of the principal reasons being that with lower pay the money would go farther and benefit more youths.

BAY STATE BATTLE

The pay issue has arisen in several areas, but the hottest disputes are probably those that have been raging in Massachusetts. Union leaders there rail at the "social workers" who, the union men claim, set up youth employment programs with low wage scales without seeking labor's views on the matter. "If we're not consulted on a program, we'll knock its damned ears off," fumes Mr. Sullivan of the Boston Labor Council.

Other Massachusetts labor officials claim that even with a $1.25-an-hour wage scale some Neighborhood Youth Corps projects threaten to deprive adults of jobs; they are particularly worried that cities might use the youthful trainees rather than higher-paid men for municipal cleanup and maintenance chores. "Instead of hiring laid-off workers as regular employes at $1.70 an hour, they might call it an antipoverty project and pay the workers $1.25," says Salvatore Camelio, President of the Massachusetts State Labor Council.

Spokesmen for antipoverty programs in Massachusetts insist Mr. Camelio's fears are groundless; they say every precaution will be taken to insure that trainees do no work that regular employes would otherwise be hired to do.

But steps are being taken to meet union objections to the low wage scales originally proposed for some Neighborhood Youth Corps projects.

Poverty program officials in Washington have now decided to require that youths in the Corps be paid at least $1.25 an hour. A New Bedford, Mass[achusetts], program has already been revised to include a flat rate of $1.25 an hour instead of a sliding scale starting as low as eighty-five cents an hour; a Boston program has been undergoing a similar re-drafting.

Embroilment in religious controversy and church-state questions poses another hazard for poverty fighters. On Jan[uary] 9th, the American Jewish Congress charged that the poverty program was violating church-state separation by allocating funds to Roman Catholic schools in several cities for special educational efforts in poor neighborhoods.

And in at least one community—Milwaukee—Catholics themselves are disturbed about the workings of the antipoverty drive. What has upset many Milwaukee Catholics is a decision by the local poverty agency to seek $50,000 of federal funds to operate birth-control clinics. Reflecting Catholic sentiment, Milwaukee's governing body, the Common Council, passed a resolution when the plan was first proposed stating that "the birth-control project is contrary to the moral code of many people in Milwaukee." *

* EDITOR'S NOTE: The OEO, however, did make the grant for the birth-control clinics.

REGIONAL POVERTY:
APPALACHIA AND THE UPPER
GREAT LAKES REGION

President's Appalachia Regional Commission and Committee on Education and Labor

The regional approach to fighting poverty was analyzed in our Introduction. The first of the two selections that follow discusses some reasons for the relatively depressed state of one important region: Appalachia, for which a $1 billion program of road-building and related economic-development aid was approved in early 1965. The second selection examines the economic distress of another, smaller, area: the three-state region of the Upper Great Lakes. The inability of the regions to adjust to changing technological or demand patterns is striking, as is the fact that, despite handicaps, the majority of their residents are not poor.

APPALACHIA

A Region Apart

Appalachia is a region apart—geographically and statistically. It is a mountain land boldly upthrust between the prosperous Eastern seaboard and the industrial Middle West—a highland region which sweeps diagonally across ten states from northern Pennsylvania to northern Alabama. Its ridges and twisted spurs and valleys measure to 165,000 square miles—an area ten times the size of Switzerland.

Appalachia has natural advantages which might normally have been the base for a thriving industrial and commercial complex. Below its surface lie some of the nation's richest mineral deposits, including the seams which have provided almost two thirds of the nation's coal supply.

From the *Report of the President's Appalachia Regional Commission*, 1964; and *Poverty in the United States*, Committee on Education and Labor, United States House of Representatives, 1964.

The region receives an annual rainfall substantially above the national average. More than three fifths of the land is forested. Its mountains offer some of the most beautiful landscapes in eastern America, readily lending themselves to tourism and recreation.

Yet this natural endowment has benefited too few of the 15.3 million people of Appalachia. The average Appalachian, whether he lives in a metropolis, in town, on the farm, or in a mountain cabin, has not matched his counterpart in the rest of the United States as a participant in the nation's economic growth.

In a region so large, there is a range of productive activity and social achievement between subregions which seems to belie the general statistics of the geographic whole. Where coal, limestone, and salt occur together, as in western West Virginia, or where the hinterland coal comes to the service of transported ore, as in northern Alabama and western Pennsylvania, industrial cities have grown. On the highland perimeter, where the valley opens, or where rivers join, other cities have emerged to serve as brokers between the resource-rich interior and the surrounding nation.

In some of these urban complexes, income and living standards far exceed the regional norm and in some cases surpass the national average. It is obvious that the problems of the rural interior counties of Appalachia cannot be equated with those of the larger cities.

But these cities, standing with one foot in Appalachia and one foot in industrial America, prosperous as they are, fall far short of the performance of urban areas in the rest of the country. They continue to reflect hard-core Appalachia's underdevelopment. For Appalachia is more striking in its homogeneity than in its diversity. Unlike though they may be, its subregions share an unhappy distinction: *rural Appalachia lags behind rural America; urban Appalachia lags behind urban America; and metropolitan Appalachia lags behind metropolitan America.*

The Legacy of Neglect

The normal process of development in a region rich in natural resources may be reduced to an A-B-C-D statement as follows:

A. Exploitation of natural resources produces local wealth.
B. That local wealth is invested in human and social capital, or so-called social overhead (the complex of housing, education, transportation, public and private services, community facilities such as hospitals, planning commissions, organizations, and institutions).

C. The investment in social overhead provides a platform for a kind of spiraling, self-generative development which is wholly independent of the natural resources that triggered the regional economy in the first place.

D. The key to sustained progress is the continuing successful development of the human and social resources attracted to the region by the natural resources.

In most of Appalachia this process was never fully realized, except in a relatively few communities. Even the first stage of exploitation of the region's great resources was retarded—by a primitive agriculture and by changing technology and consumer demand within the timber and coal industries.

The cropland was too often despoiled by agricultural practices which were not only crude but not even native. The settlers were migrants from the cities of seventeenth-century England, Ireland, and Scotland—urbanites who, during their temporary residence on coastal plantations or in the Piedmont area, had acquired the corn-and-tobacco agriculture of the Indians. This was the only kind of agriculture they knew, and they sought to establish it, first in the narrow valleys and then on the steep slopes of the highland, which the hill Indians had wisely left to the forest. It is not surprising that now almost 95 per cent of the Appalachian cropland and 70 per cent of the pastureland is in need of conservation measures.

With the construction of long-distance pipelines for oil and natural gas and with the replacement of the steam locomotive by the diesel, the exploitation of Appalachia's coal deposits was dramatically slowed. The simultaneous introduction of new machines for both underground and strip mining, drastically reducing the manpower requirements in coal mining, further aggravated the drop in regional income from that resource.

The exploitation of the great hardwood forests in the region came closest to a full development process. The huge trees were systematically felled to be processed into ties for the railroads, timbers for the mine shafts, and the lumber for eastern housing and its furniture. But when the second growth in these forests came to maturity, the railroads were built, the mines were closing, and labor-saving substitutes had taken over a substantial part of the hardwood markets in construction and furniture.

Except in its northern reaches, Appalachia was left untouched by the Ice Age, and the natural lakes which the glaciers left in other parts of the nation are largely absent in the region. Without such natural impoundments, Appalachia's runoff pours down the mountain slopes into plunging streams which periodically rise to flood entire valleys. As recently as the spring of 1963, whole sections of the region were severely flooded. The $40 million in damage which then occurred repeated a disaster of similar magnitude in 1957. There is evident need for the fostering of new public and private practices to control erosion and reduce runoff without impairing the economic benefits of agriculture, timber-cutting, and mining. Resource utilization in Appalachia can and must proceed without contributing to the tragic waste of floods.

This waste has been compounded by practices which have polluted the region's once sparkling streams and left them ugly. Acid leaked from the mines threatens fish and game. Where private plumbing facilities are lacking—as is the case in many sections of rural Appalachia—raw sewage seeps or is dumped into the waters. And the unchecked rainwater runs off the overcultivated or strip-mined slopes heavy with clay and coal dust.

Where a society depends primarily on the extraction of natural resources for its income and employment—as did the people of Appalachia —it is extremely important that a high proportion of wealth created by extraction be reinvested locally in other activities. The relatively low proportion of native capital did not produce such a reinvestment in large sections of the region. Much of the wealth produced by coal and timber was seldom seen locally. It went downstream with the great hardwood logs; it rode out on rails with the coal cars; it was mailed between distant cities as royalty checks from nonresident operators to holding companies who had bought rights to the land for fifty cents or a dollar an acre. Even the wages of local miners returned to faraway stockholders via company houses and company stores.

THE UPPER GREAT LAKES REGION

The Upper Great Lakes region is located in the northern portion of three states: Michigan, Minnesota, and Wisconsin. The Michigan counties account for 48 per cent of the region's total population; Minnesota, for one third; and Wisconsin, the remaining fifth. . . .

The area was prosperous during the period from 1890 to 1930, when its ample forest products served an insatiable eastern and Midwestern market for lumber, pulpwood, and veneers, and its high-grade iron ores fed the nation's steel mills. Now the region is faced with problems created by depletion of these two major resources: high-grade iron ore and timber. Though dairy farming has prospered, those who turned to general farming found that poor soils and a short growing season seriously limited crop production with the result that submarginal, low-production farms are abandoned or furnish only meager existence. Much of the forests have been cut over and fewer jobs are available in the forests and mines to supplement farm incomes. On the other hand, opportunities in recreation, manufacturing, trades, and services exist.

In sum, the north woods area, plundered for its timber and with depletion of rich iron ore, is sinking into poverty. Like Appalachia, the area is predominantly a one-industry area, and that industry—iron mining here, but coal mining in Appalachia—is declining. The inferior ores remaining must compete with the richer ores imported from Labrador, Venezuela, and West Africa. Copper mines now compete with more easily mined deposits in the Rocky Mountain region. New processes for converting taconite rock (20-30 per cent iron content) into 65 per cent iron-rich pellets have provided insufficient relief.

Unemployment is twice the national average, with one out of every four men unemployed in some counties. Had the area not experienced out-migration, unemployment rates might well have been much higher.

The ARA [Area Redevelopment Agency] is trying to help community leaders in their attempts to diversify the region by promoting tourism, seeking factories, and studying improved means for utilization of low-grade ores. Of the eighty counties comprising the Upper Great Lakes region, seventy-nine have been officially designated by the [U.S.] Department of Commerce as "redevelopment areas" under the Area Redevelopment Act.

An important factor contributing to the region's economic difficulties is the underutilization of its vast resources. More intensive utilization and commercial development of the area's unexploited nonmetallic mineral resources, diversification of the region's wood-products industry, and urban-development programs to attract new nonseasonal industries are needed. A major problem is also centered in the relatively low skill level of the work force. Extensive worker training which combines literary training with basic work skills is needed in order to attract new industry. In addition, more emphasis must be placed on finding new uses for basic materials produced in the area, and in the development of manufacturing industries which could then utilize these raw materials.

Michigan's Upper Peninsula. This area, an important subarea, has long been economically and culturally isolated from the great urbanized regions of the Midwest.

A heavily forested region of 10.6 million acres, it never did experience much development in agriculture. Handicaps were poor soils, a short growing season, and long distances to markets.

Economic development awaited the discovery of rich deposits of copper and iron in the mid-nineteenth century. By 1900, there were about 15,000 workers in the copper mines and another 15,000 in the iron mines. The peak in production came just before World War I with mining employment still about 30,000. Subsequently, the mining industry declined, most seriously in copper. Decline followed from the progressive exhaustion of the richer and more favorably placed ore bodies and the discovery and development of competitive ores in other regions or foreign countries.

Lumbering also brought a boom to the Upper Peninsula. In 1920 (well past the peak) production was 600 million board feet, nearly three times the present level of output.

In recent decades, even the prosperity of the war and postwar years had little impact on the Upper Peninsula. The population of 306,000 in 1960 was 6 per cent less than it was fifty years ago. Unemployment and underemployment are chronic problems.

Other Viewpoints on What Government Should and Should Not Do

POVERTY AND PECKSNIFF

Irving Kristol

As the title of his article suggests, Irving Kristol is sharply critical of many who support the War on Poverty. An advocate of minimal government participation in the economy, Kristol attacks what he regards as the exaggerations and distortions of the poverty problem. He rejects attempts to help the poor by means other than increasing their after-tax cash income. Irving Kristol has been editor of Encounter, The Reporter, *and of* Basic Books, Inc.

In order to appreciate just how odd an enterprise the Johnson Administration's "war on poverty" is, let us consider the following two facts:

1. While the Administration has expressed the profoundest concern for those with incomes under the poverty level of $3000 a year, it is simultaneously engaged in taking money out of their pockets. Not surreptitiously, and not accidentally, but by means of the federal income tax. Even after one takes the recent tax reduction into account, a childless couple earning $2800 a year (and assuming the standard deductions) pays $264 in tax; a couple with one child pays $140; a couple with two children pays $20. Nevertheless, none of the government officials who are designing ingenious schemes (and issuing eloquent press releases) for the alleviation of poverty has breathed the faintest suggestion that this state of affairs is in any way paradoxical.

2. Though the statistics make it clear that just about one half of those below the $3000 poverty level are elderly people or are families with no male head, the government has made no movement whatsover—and the ideologists of the "war on poverty" are themselves not even demanding

it—to raise Social Security benefits,* widows' pensions, and aid to dependent children. This is, after all, a simple matter: One need only pass a law. It is not even a very expensive proposition: The windfall which employers and workers have just received as a result of the tax cut would finance a truly whopping raise in such payments. Nor does the idea violate any sound economic principles: if one wants to spur on the economy, it surely makes sense to allocate purchasing power to those who, having the greatest obvious need, will most obviously spend their money rather than save it. Yet President Johnson, in his recent speech to officials of the Internal Revenue Service, declared that, in order to reduce the number of those below the poverty level by one half, a long, intense, and arduous campaign would be necessary. I do not know of a single commentator or editorial writer who pointed out that he was in error—that, in fact, this particular operation could be successfully completed in practically no time at all, and without much real inconvenience to anyone.

Now, I do not think that the Administration's "war on poverty" is merely a hypocritical and callous publicity stunt. There is, to be sure, a strong odor of hucksterism about it: one might recall that, simultaneous with its declaration of war against poverty, the Administration set up a new commission to recommend action by the federal government that would reduce the incidence of heart disease, cancer, and strokes. But I prefer to believe that this hucksterism is a surface affair, the usual political froth, and that the reason the Administration is behaving so oddly is that it has been led—I should say, misled—into trying to encompass a most complicated reality with the aid of a few simple clichés and slogans. As a consequence, it has confused the issues, and itself.

This confusion is evident in practically all the journalism devoted to the "war on poverty," in such tracts as Michael Harrington's *The Other America,* and in many of the letters that *The New Leader* has received after my last article appeared. For instance, there is a constant (and, in Harrington's case, a willful) confusion between the problem of unemployment—especially technological unemployment—and the problem of poverty. As A. H. Raskin points out (and as I have argued too, in previous columns) the question of technological unemployment is as serious as it is perplexing. But technological unemployment is one problem, and poverty is another. They do overlap, of course—but not so much as one might think. *Only one sixteenth of all poor families* (i.e., with incomes under $3000) *are headed by an unemployed person.* Even were

---

* EDITOR'S NOTE: Social Security benefits were raised in 1965, at the same time that the "Medicare" Program was adopted.

we, by some miracle, to abolish technological (or any other kind of) unemployment, we should have made little dent in the problem of poverty.
. . . [Because] people like Mike Harrington and Ben Seligman seem determined to misunderstand me—nothing personal, I'm sure: they misunderstand everyone who has the temerity to disagree with them—I suppose I had better say, in so many words, that I am *against* technological unemployment, that I have no desire to minimize its hardships and its terrors, and that I believe it to be a problem of the first magnitude for American society. The only point I am making here is that the identification of the problems of unemployment and poverty is sterile and misleading. Yet this identification is now the common coin of American journalism: Witness the way practically every writer on the subject slides from the subject of poverty to such topics as rehabilitation, retraining, re-education—as if the latter represented *a solution* to the former. (Something tells me I had better not leave this paragraph without stating explicitly that I have nothing *against* rehabilitation, retraining, re-education, and so on, for those who can benefit from such programs. The President's idea for a ccc [Civilian Conservation Corps] * that will enroll unemployed dropouts is a good idea. Insofar as the Administration's "war on poverty" boils down to this sort of thing, it is commendable enough—but it is not anything like a war against poverty.)

While on the subject of misunderstanding, I should like to report my astonishment at the number of people who have taken moral umbrage at my statement that "the poor in America are not an oppressed social class but a statistical segment." Harrington quotes this, and refers to my "main thesis that the American poor are a product of mathematical juggling rather than social reality." Now, I should have thought it clear enough that a "statistical *segment*" is not the same thing as a "statistical *illusion*." What I intended to say—what, in fact, I did say—was that the American poor are a heterogeneous group; that they are not a permanent body, but one which is constantly recruiting new members and losing old ones; that the causes of their poverty are both diverse and complicated; that there is no single, radical "solution" to their difficulties; and that this is the kind of problem that does not automatically succumb to a sweeping declaration of war by politicians and publicists.

I do not doubt that the poor are with us; and . . . [because] I happen to live on New York's West Side, I do not need—as Mike Harrington so dashingly recommends—to take a subway ride, in order to discover them.

* EDITOR'S NOTE: In the language of the Economic Opportunity Act, this is the Job Corps.

(Nor can I follow Seligman's kind advice to "drive off the turnpikes" the next time I take a trip, as I neither own a car nor know how to drive one.) Whether the poor will *always* be with us, and just how large a proportion of the population they do and will constitute, are other matters. Here I think it is the ideologists of the "war on poverty" who are guilty of statistical juggling.

It is an incontestable fact that families with incomes under $4000 a year—in fixed, 1962 dollars, i.e., taking into account the intervening rise in prices (some of my correspondents seem not to have understood that all of my figures made allowances for the decreased purchasing power of the dollar)—fell from 60 per cent of the population in 1929 to 23 per cent today. I regard this as a considerable accomplishment, and one that the American polity has every right to take pride in. It goes without saying that one has no right to be smug about it; there is no such thing as a right to be smug. But why is it a sign of callousness to mention this fact, and a sign of keen moral sensitivity to fudge it, distort it, or disbelieve it?

And fudge, distort, and disbelieve it the ideologists of poverty do, most promiscuously. Mainly they do it by blandly confusing the question of poverty with the question of the distribution of wealth—i.e., by defining as "poor" all those who are in the lower fifth, or fourth, or third of the income pyramid. All of these people are indisputably *poorer* than the rest of their fellow Americans; but not all of them are poor in the conventional dictionary sense ("having little or nothing in the way of wealth, goods, or means of subsistence"), and only a minority are poor in comparison with the *average* American of thirty years ago.

A few weeks ago, one of the best of the British correspondents in this country began a long dispatch from Washington as follows: "This is the richest country in the world. Yet at least a fifth of its citizens are poor *by any standards*." (My italics.) Deep down, he must have known this was false even as he wrote it: Nothing like a fifth of our citizens are poor by *British* standards. But I do not question his good faith. Overexposure to propaganda about "the war on poverty" had simply ruined his perspective.

But don't we, as a progressive society, wish to raise our standard of poverty as the general standard of living rises? Yes, of course we do. But let us not then promptly forget that we have given a new meaning to the term poverty! Let us not take advantage of unnoticed ambiguities in the word to strike moral postures and grab headlines with resounding accusations against our American democracy for being nothing but an affluent superstructure on a base of mass misery. Let us not indulge in polemical sophistry, as Leon Keyserling does when he blithely assumes that all the houses owned, and all the apartments rented, by families below the $3000 income level are shacks or slums (it is not so). . . . And let us not fall victim to the curious myopia of a Paul Jacobs, who was sent out to explore poorest America by a high-minded foundation, and who returned with the horrifying news (solemnly quoted in *Newsweek*) that "they eat meat, and potatoes, and gravy—whoever heard of a fruit or a salad?" Paul Jacobs is, I happen to know, an admirable connoisseur of salads. But, for most of us, "let them eat meat" is not exactly the slogan we associate with a heartless *ancien régime*.

Yes, the poor are with us. John Kenneth Galbraith has been much maligned by those who, having read the title, seem to think his *The Affluent Society* denies the existence of poverty in the United States. In fact, his thesis was that poverty had changed its social character, that the category of "the poor" is no longer (as it used to be) identical with the category "working class." Instead, what we have, mainly, are "case poverty" (the old, the sick, and so on) and "island poverty" (depressed areas). Neither of these poverties lend[s itself] . . . easily to ideological crusades for the reformation of the social order. And that is why, I suspect, the ideologists of the "war on poverty" are so eager to blur distinctions, ignore obvious facts, and exaggerate the implications of their statistical findings. It is precisely a crusade for the reformation of the social order, and no mere alleviation of poverty or misery, that they most deeply hunger for.

Ever since the end of the New Deal, and the close of World War II, the United States has been a land of festering and frustrated idealism. Somehow, all the old moral and political certainties had lost their truth and their power. Somehow, all the large ideological questions seemed to get converted into a thousand intricate, thorny, and intractable little technical questions. For a while, the ideology of foreign aid seemed an adequate substitute—we were going to abolish world poverty and create a world democracy by offering our money and our "know-how" to the underdeveloped nations. Well, that whole movement has dribbled away into an interminable series of quarrels over the scope of such aid, the specific utility or disutility of such aid, the management of such aid, etc. Now the ideology of poverty has come along as a suitable vehicle for the constellation of petty resentments, glib righteousness, and selfless enthusiasm that have always characterized American reform movements. It is conceivable that the existence of this frustrated idealism may yet be a more serious social and political problem for democracy in the United States than the existence of poverty itself.

There are already a few signs that the crusade against poverty is turning unpleasantly sour, as the complexities of the problem slowly unman the ideological simplicities of the reformers. Indeed, there are moments when one wonders whether we are witnessing a war against poverty or a war against the poor. Exasperation with the poor for being of so little help in solving the problem of poverty is gradually replacing abstract compassion. Already several voices have been heard to say that the way to handle the young dropouts is to shove them into the Armed Forces—where, presumably, a tough sergeant will accomplish what teacher could not. And a forthcoming Twentieth Century Fund study on "Poverty in the Affluent Society" will suggest that welfare payments be made contingent on the recipient's willingness to go back to school, or relocate, or do whatever the social worker in charge thinks is in the national interest.

None of this is really surprising (or ought to be). The one element that has always been singularly lacking in the "war on poverty" is a sense of humanity, as contrasted to mere humanitarianism. In my original *New Leader* article I recommended that, under the present circumstances, the most meaningful gesture would be simply to give poor people more money—either through increased Social Security and allied payments, or through some such scheme as Milton Friedman's "negative income tax." (Those with annual incomes under $3000 would receive "refunds" to bring them above that level.) From the opprobrium that was directed against me, as a result of making this suggestion, one would have thought I had urged that money be *taken* from the poor. How, my correspondents angrily asked, would cash payments help break "the vicious circle of poverty"? I don't know the answer to that question; and neither do they. The retraining, re-education, and rehabilitation programs they set so much store by will break this vicious circle for some. But it is fairly clear by now, as indicated by the experience of the past couple of years, that these will constitute a minority. In any case, what is the relevance of all this pseudosociological talk about the vicious circle of poverty for the aged, the physically and mentally sick, the widowed, the abandoned? They don't need re-education, nor can they possibly benefit from it. All they need is money.

Will they spend this money wisely? I don't know, and I don't really much care. So far as I am concerned it is *their* money, and they are free to spend it as they see fit. If they prefer a color television set to an indoor toilet, that's their business. Only an officious know-it-all can presume to decide what will make a happy life for everyone else. I have enough trouble trying, without much success, to figure out what will make a happy life for me.

I do not doubt the genuineness of Mike Harrington's hatred of poverty.

I only wish he were a little more respectful to the poor—the undeserving poor as well as the deserving, re-educable, retrainable, rehabilitatable poor. For me, one of the most striking features of his book is the rhetoric of slander that he unwittingly lapses into when he talks of poor people. In Mike Harrington's America, there are 40-50 million people who are "maimed in body and spirit"—all because they have incomes under $4000 a year. Well, that's not my America, and I don't believe it's the America of most of the 40-50 million, either. There are plenty of poor who manage—some routinely, some heroically—to lead dignified, decent, and humanly satisfying lives. They are, in my opinion, entitled to more money than they have; they are not getting a "fair share" of the affluent society. They are entitled to have every possible opportunity to move upward on our socioeconomic scale, if they wish to. But they are also entitled not to be hectored, badgered, sermonized, psychoanalyzed, fingerprinted, Rohrschached, and generally bossed around by a self-appointed body of self-anointed redeemers—who are, in any case, less interested in helping poor people than in satisfying some particular ideological passion.

PROPOSED POLICIES AND PROGRAMS: PLANNING A LONG-RANGE BALANCED EFFORT

Leon H. Keyserling

There are many views of how to eliminate poverty and, in particular, what the role of the federal government should be. Leon Keyserling, former Chairman of the CEA and currently President of the Conference on Economic Progress, favors an extensive government role in antipoverty efforts. His proposals are numerous, ranging from increased public assistance and unemployment benefits to comprehensive health insurance, aid for education, tax reform, and stimulatory fiscal policy to speed economic growth.

This chapter lists all proposals in this study. . . . The listing cannot be in order of importance, for they are links in a chain no stronger than the weakest, and many of the proposed programs overlap. Nor is it feasible to list programs according to the groups which they are intended to help; many programs converge upon the same individuals. The chain is designed, in lifting people out of poverty, to improve the tone of our whole social and moral performance.

THE MOST GENERAL MEASURES: NATIONAL FISCAL AND MONETARY POLICIES

Federal tax policy. For economic and social reasons, any further tax reduction should concentrate upon enlarging the after-tax income of low- and lower-middle-income families and unattached individuals. This could be accomplished by lifting exemption credits in the personal income tax structure—these ought to be approximately doubled—and by reduction of federal excise or sales taxes on necessities as distinguished from luxuries.

From *Progress or Poverty*, by Leon H. Keyserling. Reprinted by permission of the Conference on Economic Progress and Leon H. Keyserling.

Federal spending policies. Increased federal spending should take high precedence over further tax reduction. Wisely directed spending is obviously more helpful to the poor. And viewing the new technology and automation, spending can also do much more to help everybody—and especially the poor—because of its much greater stimulus to those types of output which will add most to employment opportunity and economic growth. . . .

Monetary policies. The monetary policy prevalent since 1952 has been highly regressive in its income effects, as higher interest payments have penalized low-income groups. And tight money has worked severely against adequate employment and economic growth. The policies of the Federal Reserve Board should be drastically revised—by Congressional and/or Presidential intervention—toward a more liberal expansion of the money supply from year to year, with lower interest rates.

MEASURES TO RESHAPE THE STRUCTURE OF JOB OPPORTUNITY: PRIME IMPORTANCE OF HOUSING AND URBAN RENEWAL

Because of the new technology and automation, the rate of productivity gains in agriculture and in many branches of industry is extremely rapid. Even though a greatly increased demand for the products of these types of economic activity is essential toward lifting the consumption standards of the poor and deprived, feasible increases in such demand are unlikely to outrun by much the further productivity gains in agriculture and in these branches of industry. This means relatively small opportunities for expansion of employment in these types of economic activity. By far the most promising opportunities to expand employment—especially among the unskilled and semiskilled—are in the types of economic activity where our unmet nationwide needs call for expansion of goods and services far in excess of the likely technological advances in such types of activity. And in addition to the employment benefits which would result from vast expansion of such types of activity, the goods and services which such types of activity would turn out would also be exceedingly helpful to the poor as consumers. This calls for vigorous measures to reshape the entire structure of production, demand, and job opportunity.

Housing and urban renewal is by far the most important of these areas quantitatively, and as important as any qualitatively. We need to lift housing starts from 1.6 million (almost all for middle- and high-income groups) in 1963 to about 2.2 million by 1970, with almost half of these starts divided equally between lower-middle- and low-income groups. This effort will require more favorable credit terms, including lower interest rates, to stimulate private investment in housing; for the poverty-stricken people in the slums, it will require a vast increase in public outlays at all levels, especially by the federal government. This housing expansion should be accompanied by enormous programs of urban renewal. . . .

Conventional-type public works, to serve genuine needs and to reduce unemployment, should receive at least $1 billion a year of additional federal support.

DIRECT INCOME-REINFORCEMENT PROGRAMS

Minimum-wage protection. The glaring deficiencies in coverage under the Federal Fair Labor Standards Act should be remedied promptly, and the minimum wage floor in general should be lifted to $2.00 an hour. Overtime premiums should be extended and liberalized.

Unemployment insurance. By combined state and federal action, including higher federal standards and some federal contributions, unemployment insurance should as soon as feasible become the right of all those unemployed through no fault of their own, for as long as they are unemployed, and at average benefit payments of at least half the average full-time working wage. Regular insurance benefits should be reinforced by special revolving funds and installment payments to laid-off workers. With increased federal aid, disability coverage under public assistance and OASDI [Old-Age, Survivors', and Disability Insurance] should be as broad as the broadened coverage under unemployment insurance, and disability benefits should be lifted to adequate standards as to amounts and duration.

Farm-income improvement. The whole national farm program needs drastic reconstruction, to focus more effectively upon the goal of income parity rather than price parity for farmers, and to get more of the income increases to those farmers who need them most, with accent upon the family-type farm. Hired farm labor should be covered by minimum-wage and unemployment-insurance legislation, and should have the right to organize and bargain collectively. . . .

Old-age insurance and pensions. These programs, almost everywhere, are woefully behind the times, and this has grave effects upon the lives of the poor. Within about five years, the average benefits under OASDI should be approximately doubled, taking into account not only retired workers but also their spouses or survivors and other dependents. Emphasis should also be placed upon earlier retirements in general, special forms of early-retirement benefits, and pension-reinsurance plans. Because of the regressive nature of payroll taxes, federal contributions financed by general taxation should assume a large part of the costs of benefit payments under OASDI. With increased federal aid, the same retirement and income objectives should be sought for our senior citizens and their families who are helped by pensions rather than insurance, and for those who for one reason or another receive neither. There is room for very large improvement in those aspects of OASDI which deal, not with old-age benefits proper, but with other types of help—including medical—to those in great need.

Workmen's compensation. There is urgent need for very large improvements in benefits and coverage under state workmen's compensation laws; the time has come to consider federal standards and aid to expedite this process.

Special and general public assistance. One of the greatest tragedies of our national life is the pitiful inadequacy of all types of public assistance (both monetary and in kind) to broken families in need, to families headed by women who cannot work, and to many other types of family groups living in poverty. This calls for enlarged federal assistance to those special types of state and local public assistance now aided federally to a degree, coupled with initiation of federal aid to general public assistance. . . .

PROGRAMS TO BUILD OUR HUMAN RESOURCES

These programs would have the same double-barrelled effects as the proposed housing programs. They would serve immediately and directly the needs of the poor. And because the needed increases in output in these areas would far exceed the rate of technological gains in these areas, these programs would do most to enlarge employment opportunity, and, in their construction aspects, would do most to increase employment opportunity for the unskilled and semiskilled.

Education. In the public schools alone, we need from now through 1970 about 100,000 new classrooms a year, compared with actual building programs averaging about 60,000. We need to recruit about 100,000 teachers a year for the public schools, or about 50 per cent more than recent and current recruitment levels. Teachers still need large salary increases, especially in the poorer states. Specialized programs to deal with the school dropouts should be pushed vigorously. In higher education, very large increases are needed in scholarships, student loans, and physical plant. . . .

Medical care. Prompt enactment of Medicare is essential, along with expansion of other types of public medical assistance to the needy regardless of age. We need approximately to double the average annual rate of hospital construction during the next ten years, along with vast increases in the numbers of doctors and nurses, and their improved distribution throughout the country. Medical research has made great strides, but it needs far more support. . . .

TRAINING AND RETRAINING PROGRAMS

The very encouraging projection of training and retraining programs for the poor and deprived under the Economic Opportunity Act of 1964 leaves many needs untouched. Handicapped workers need more attention. Federal aid in the form of relocation allowances is essential. . . .

CONSERVATION AND IMPROVEMENT OF OUR NATURAL RESOURCES

We have been experiencing a long drawn out neglect in this whole field. In some areas, water and power supplies are lagging far behind very rapid population growth and corresponding industrial growth. The rivers flowing through some of our most congested urban areas are polluted. The air hanging over many of our industrial areas is dirty and foul. Recreational facilities and areas are inadequate and inaccessible, certainly for many of the poor and deprived. Atomic energy research and development for industrial purposes should be quickened, with more emphasis upon public control or regulation in the public interest. Such investment is an essential part of the expansion of employment opportunity, especially for the lesser-skilled who comprise so large a portion of those who are poor, young, and jobless. This is basically a national responsibility. . . .

PROGRAMS FOR THE DISTRESSED AREAS

Our approaches thus far to the shocking conditions in Appalachia and elsewhere are mere nibbling on the fringes. With appropriate modifications, we need to apply to these areas the same boldness and practical imagination, and the same comprehensiveness of effort, which went into the making of TVA. Our country now sorely needs many TVA's.

REDRESSING DISLOCATIONS CAUSED
BY GOVERNMENT PROGRAMS

Shifts in the size and location of national defense activities, as well as in government procurement activities arising under other programs, result in major changes in employment opportunity. The government should make every effort to reduce dislocating effects to a minimum, including placement of new plants and other activities in labor-surplus rather than in labor-shortage areas, and curtailment of plants and other activities in labor-shortage rather than in labor-surplus areas. Similarly, the international trade and tariff policies of the United States have a short-range adverse impact upon some industries and employment therein. As these international policies are in the national interest, their economic costs should be borne by the nation rather than by specific groups, and compensatory action of the proper kind should be taken to prevent these policies from impacting with excessive severity upon these particular groups.

THE WAR AGAINST DISCRIMINATION IN ALL ITS FORMS

We cannot rest on our oars with respect to civil rights and liberties. These rights and liberties are precious for their own sake; their denial in any degree is evidence of the man-made oppression and neglect which also filter through the whole problem of poverty and deprivation in our country. Further, the whole crusade for civil rights and liberties needs to be allied with the whole crusade against poverty; for even when people become entirely free, they will still struggle to be well fed and well housed. Other forms of discrimination, . . . [although] less talked about, are also on the scene. Despite passage of highly desirable legislation by the Congress in 1964, women are still grossly discriminated against— in their education and training opportunities, their chances to get jobs, and their pay when on the job. Through combined action at all levels, this type of discrimination should be stamped out. The same comments apply to the irrational and unjust aspects of discrimination based on age.

THE RANGE OF STATE AND LOCAL RESPONSIBILITIES

Superficially, it might seem that the foregoing listing would impose too heavy a share of the war against poverty upon the federal government. But to date, the states and localities have made Herculean efforts to expand their services, in sharp contrast with inadequate action at the federal level. In an article in the September 1964 *Harper's*, Edmund G. Brown, the governor of our most populous state [California] with one of the most intricate combinations of every kind of social and economic problem, sets forth courageously and admirably the fallacy of denying that such problems as medical care, poverty, and education are national in scope, or asserting that they fall within "the province of the city or state just because they occur in the city or the state." Governor Brown points out that we live in a time of "Jet-Age federalism and it is here to stay, no matter how fervently its detractors invoke the Founding Fathers."

THE NEED FOR IMPROVED UTILIZATION OF THE EMPLOYMENT ACT OF 1946

The very real problem is how we may obtain the knowledge and consents required for the best attainable blend of private and public efforts at all levels. The Employment Act of 1946 is admirably suited to this purpose. But operations under this Act, . . . [although] rewarding in many respects, require further improvement.

The Economic Reports of the President should include the types of goals set forth in this study but not as yet adequately spelled out in these *Reports*. They should contain a *Job Budget*, looking at least five—and probably ten—years ahead. As part of their analysis of purchasing power, and of the policies needed to maximize it, they should embrace the objective of *a minimum-adequacy level of living for all American families, and include goals for the rate of the reduction of poverty in America.* Only these *Reports* can carry to a logical conclusion the coordination of the war against poverty intended by the responsibilities vested in the director under the Economic Opportunity Act of 1964; the programs under his purview are at best limited segments of a total war against poverty. The *Economic Reports* should include the equivalent of the *American Economic Performance Budget* used throughout this study to develop balanced goals. The federal budget should become an integral part of this *American Economic Performance Budget*—for national fiscal policy is only an implement of national economic and social policy— and so should our other basic national economic programs, such as Social Security, housing, and monetary policies.

THE RANGE OF STATE, LOCAL, AND PRIVATE RESPONSIBILITIES

Superficially, it might seem that the foregoing listing would impose too heavy a share of the war against poverty upon the federal government. But the projections in this study urge that proposed increases in outlays at the state and local level, comparing 1975 with 1963, be more than six sevenths as large as those proposed for the federal budget. And there is nothing in the study which indicates the prospect or desirability of any shrinkage in the traditional role and responsibilities of private enterprise. . . . [Although] the study urges, comparing 1975 with 1963, an increase of [$]77.4 billion in the annual rate of outlays for goods and services by governments at all levels, it projects an increase of [$]103.6 billion in gross private investment (including net foreign), and an increase of [$]335 billion in private consumer expenditures, adding up to an increase of [$]516 billion in the annual rate of total national production. Further, the proposals for expansion of Social Security would impose additional obligations in the form of payroll taxes upon employers and workers in the private sector, even though federal legislation would continue to provide the framework.

ALLEVIATION OF POVERTY

Milton Friedman

Milton Friedman's solution to the poverty problem is a "negative in-
come tax." Under his proposal, cash payments would be made to the poor
through the existing tax mechanism. A powerful spokesman for indi-
vidual initiative and a minimal role for government, Friedman is Pro-
fessor of Economics at the University of Chicago, and author of Essays
in Positive Economics *and* A Theory of the Consumption Function. *He*
was a principal economic advisor to Senator Barry Goldwater during the
1964 Presidential campaign.

ALLEVIATION OF POVERTY

The extraordinary economic growth experienced by Western countries
during the past two centuries and the wide distribution of the benefits
of free enterprise have enormously reduced the extent of poverty in any
absolute sense in the capitalistic countries of the West. But poverty is in
part a relative matter, and even in these countries, there are clearly many
people living under conditions that the rest of us label *poverty*.

One recourse, and in many ways the most desirable, is private charity.
It is noteworthy that the heyday of laissez-faire, the middle and late
nineteenth century in Britain and the United States, saw an extraordinary
proliferation of private eleemosynary organizations and institutions. One
of the major costs of the extension of governmental welfare activities has
been the corresponding decline in private charitable activities.

It can be argued that private charity is insufficient because the benefits from it accrue to people other than those who make the gifts—again,
a neighborhood effect. I am distressed by the sight of poverty; I am

benefited by its alleviation; but I am benefited equally whether I or someone else pays for its alleviation; the benefits of other people's charity therefore partly accrue to me. To put it differently, we might all of us be willing to contribute to the relief of poverty, *provided* everyone else did. We might not be willing to contribute the same amount without such assurance. In small communities, public pressure can suffice to realize the proviso even with private charity. In the large impersonal communities that are increasingly coming to dominate our society, it is much more difficult for it to do so.

Suppose one accepts, as I do, this line of reasoning as justifying governmental action to alleviate poverty—to set, as it were, a floor under the standard of life of every person in the community. There remain the questions: How much? and How? I see no way of deciding "how much" except in terms of the amount of taxes we—by which I mean the great bulk of us—are willing to impose on ourselves for the purpose. The question, "How?" affords more room for speculation.

Two things seem clear. First, if the objective is to alleviate poverty, we should have a program directed at helping the poor. There is every reason to help the poor man who happens to be a farmer—not because he is a farmer, but because he is poor. The program, that is, should be designed to help people as people, not as members of particular occupational groups or age groups or wage-rate groups or labor organizations or industries. This is a defect of farm programs, general old-age benefits, minimum-wage laws, pro-union legislation, tariffs, licensing provisions of crafts or professions, and so on in seemingly endless profusion. Second, so far as possible the program should, while operating through the market, not distort the market or impede its functioning. This is a defect of price supports, minimum-wage laws, tariffs, and the like.

The arrangement that recommends itself on purely mechanical grounds is a negative income tax. We now have an exemption of $600 per person under the federal income tax (plus a minimum 10 per cent flat deduction*). If an individual receives $100 taxable income—i.e., an income of $100 in excess of the exemption and deductions, he pays tax. Under the proposal, if his taxable income minus $100—i.e., $100 less than the exemption plus deductions—he would pay a negative tax—i.e., receive a subsidy. If the rate of subsidy were, say, 50 per cent, he would receive $50. If he had no income at all—and, for simplicity, no deductions—and

---

* EDITOR'S NOTE: Under the 1964 changes in income-tax legislation, a floor of $300 plus $100 for each dependent was added to the 10 per cent deduction. Thus, a family of four would have a minimum deduction of either $600 or 10 per cent of its income, whichever was larger. This minimum deduction is in addition to the personal exemption of $600 per person.

the rate were constant, he would receive $300. He might receive more than this if he had deductions, for example, for medical expenses, so that his income less deductions was negative even before subtracting the exemption. The rates of subsidy could, of course, be graduated just as the rates of tax above the exemption are. In this way, it would be possible to set a floor below which no man's net income (defined now to include the subsidy) could fall—in the simple example, $300 per person. The precise floor set would depend on what the community could afford.

The advantages of this arrangement are clear. It is directed specifically at the problem of poverty. It gives help in the form most useful to the individual—namely, cash. It is general and could be substituted for the host of special measures now in effect. It makes explicit the cost borne by society. It operates outside the market. Like any other measures to alleviate poverty, it reduces the incentives of those helped to help themselves, but it does not eliminate that incentive entirely, as a system of supplementing incomes up to some fixed minimum would. An extra dollar earned always means more money available for expenditure.

No doubt there would be problems of administration, but these seem to me a minor disadvantage, if they be a disadvantage at all. The system would fit directly into our current income tax system and could be administered along with it. The present tax system covers the bulk of income recipients and the necessity of covering all would have the by-product of improving the operation of the present income tax. More important, if enacted as a substitute for the present ragbag of measures directed at the same end, the total administrative burden would surely be reduced.

A few brief calculations suggest also that this proposal could be far less costly in money, let alone in the degree of governmental intervention involved, than our present collection of welfare measures. Alternatively, these calculations can be regarded as showing how wasteful our present measures are, judged as measures for helping the poor.

In 1961, government [expenditures] amounted to something like $33 billion (federal, state, and local) on direct welfare payments and programs of all kinds: old-age assistance, Social Security benefit payments, aid to dependent children, general assistance, farm price-support programs, public housing, and so on. I have excluded veterans' benefits in making this calculation. I have also made no allowance for the direct and indirect costs of such measures as minimum-wage laws, tariffs, licensing provisions, and so on, or for the costs of public health activities, state and local expenditures on hospitals, mental institutions, and the like.

There are approximately 57 million consumer units (unattached in-

dividuals and families) in the United States. The 1961 expenditures of
$33 billion would have financed outright cash grants of nearly $6000
per consumer unit to the 10 per cent with the lowest incomes. Such
grants would have raised their incomes above the average for all units in
the United States. Alternatively, these expenditures would have financed
grants of nearly $3000 per consumer unit to the 20 per cent with the
lowest incomes. Even if one went so far as that one third whom New
Dealers were fond of calling ill-fed, ill-housed, and ill-clothed, 1961 expenditures would have financed grants of nearly $2000 per consumer
unit—roughly the sum which, after allowing for the change in the level
of prices, was the income which separated the lower one third in the
middle 1930s from the upper two thirds. Today, fewer than one eighth
of consumer units have an income, adjusted for the change in the level
of prices, as low as that of the lowest third in the middle 1930s.

Clearly, these are all far more extravagant programs than can be
justified to "alleviate poverty" even by a rather generous interpretation
of that term. A program which *supplemented* the incomes of the 20
per cent of the consumer units with the lowest incomes so as to raise
them to the lowest income of the rest would cost less than half of what
we are now spending.

The major disadvantage of the proposed negative income tax is its
political implications. It establishes a system under which taxes are imposed on some to pay subsidies to others. And presumably, these others
have a vote. There is always the danger that instead of being an arrangement under which the great majority tax themselves willingly to help
an unfortunate minority, it will be converted into one under which a
majority imposes taxes for its own benefit on an unwilling minority.
Because this proposal makes the process so explicit, the danger is perhaps greater than with other measures. I see no solution to this problem except to rely on the self-restraint and goodwill of the electorate.

Liberalism and Egalitarianism

The heart of the liberal philosophy is a belief in the dignity of the
individual, in his freedom to make the most of his capacities and opportunities according to his own lights, subject only to the proviso that he
not interfere with the freedom of other individuals to do the same. This
implies a belief in the equality of men in one sense; in their inequality
in another. Each man has an equal right to freedom. This is an important
and fundamental right precisely because men are different, because one
man will want to do different things with his freedom than another, and

in the process can contribute more than another to the general culture of the society in which many men live.

The liberal will therefore distinguish sharply between equality of rights and equality of opportunity, on the one hand, and material equality or equality of outcome on the other. He may welcome the fact that a free society in fact tends toward greater material equality than any other yet tried. But he will regard this as a desirable byproduct of a free society, not its major justification. He will welcome measures that promote both freedom and equality—such as measures to eliminate monopoly power and to improve the operation of the market. He will regard private charity directed at helping the less fortunate as an example of the proper use of freedom. And he may approve state action toward ameliorating poverty as a more effective way in which the great bulk of the community can achieve a common objective. He will do so with regret, however, at having to substitute compulsory for voluntary action.

The egalitarian will go this far, too. But he will want to go further. He will defend taking from some to give to others, not as a more effective means whereby the "some" can achieve an objective they want to achieve, but on grounds of "justice." At this point, equality comes sharply into conflict with freedom; one must choose. One cannot be both an egalitarian, in this sense, and a liberal.

SOCIAL WELFARE MEASURES

Measures intended to help the poor sometimes actually hurt them. Milton Friedman argues that this has been the case with such social welfare measures as public housing, minimum-wage laws, and farm price supports.

The humanitarian and egalitarian sentiment which helped produce the steeply graduated individual income tax has also produced a host of other measures directed at promoting the "welfare" of particular groups. The most important single set of measures is the bundle misleadingly labeled *Social Security*. Others are public housing, minimum-wage laws, farm price supports, medical care for particular groups, special aid programs, and so on. . . .

SOCIAL WELFARE MEASURES

Public Housing

One argument frequently made for public housing is based on an alleged neighborhood effect: slum districts in particular, and other low-quality housing to a lesser degree, are said to impose higher costs on the community in the form of fire and police protection. This literal neighborhood effect may well exist. But insofar as it does, it alone argues, not for public housing, but for higher taxes on the kind of housing that adds to social costs . . . [because] this would tend to equalize private and social cost.

It will be answered at once that the extra taxes would bear on low-income people and that this is undesirable. The answer means that public housing is proposed not on the ground of neighborhood effects but as a means of helping low-income people. If this be the case, why subsidize housing in particular? If funds are to be used to help the poor, would they not be used more effectively by being given in cash rather than in kind? Surely, the families being helped would rather have a given sum in cash than in the form of housing. They could themselves spend the money on housing if they so desired. Hence, they would never be worse off if given cash; if they regarded other needs as more important, they would be better off. The cash subsidy would solve the neighborhood effect as well as the subsidy in kind, . . . [because] if it were not used to buy housing it would be available to pay extra taxes justified by the neighborhood effect.

Public housing cannot therefore be justified on the grounds either of neighborhood effects or of helping poor families. It can be justified, if at all, only on grounds of paternalism; that the families being helped "need" housing more than they "need" other things but would themselves either not agree or would spend the money unwisely. The liberal will be inclined to reject this argument for responsible adults. He cannot completely reject it in the more indirect form in which it affects children; namely, that parents will neglect the welfare of the children, who "need" the better housing. But he will surely demand evidence much more persuasive and to the point than the kind usually given before he can accept this final argument as adequate justification for large expenditures on public housing.

So much could have been said in the abstract, in advance of actual experience with public housing. Now that we have had experience, we can go much farther. In practice, public housing has turned out to have effects very different indeed from those intended.

Far from improving the housing of the poor, as its proponents expected, public housing has done just the reverse. The number of dwelling units destroyed in the course of erecting public housing projects has been far larger than the number of new dwelling units constructed. But public housing as such has done nothing to reduce the number of persons to be housed. The effect of public housing has therefore been to raise the number of persons per dwelling unit. Some families have probably been better housed than they would otherwise have been—those who were fortunate enough to get occupancy of the publicly built units. But this has only made the problem for the rest all the worse, . . . [because] the average density of all together went up.

Of course, private enterprise offset[s] some of the deleterious effect of the public housing program by conversion of existing quarters and construction of new ones for either the persons directly displaced or, more generally, the persons displaced at one or two removes in the game of musical chairs set in motion by the public housing projects. However, these private resources would have been available in the absence of the public housing program.

Why did the public housing program have this effect? For the general reason we have stressed time and again. The general interest that motivated many to favor instituting the program is diffuse and transitory. Once the program was adopted, it was bound to be dominated by the special interests that it could serve. In this case, the special interests were those local groups that were anxious to have blighted areas cleared and refurbished, either because they owned property there or because the blight was threatening local or central business districts. Public housing served as a convenient means to accomplish their objective, which required more destruction than construction. Even so, "urban blight" is still with us in undiminished force, to judge by the growing pressure for federal funds to deal with it.

Another gain its proponents expected from public housing was the reduction of juvenile delinquency by improving housing conditions. Here again, the program in many instances had precisely the opposite effect, entirely aside from its failure to improve *average* housing conditions. The income limitations quite properly imposed for the occupancy of public housing at subsidized rentals have led to a very high density of "broken" families—in particular, divorced or widowed mothers with children. Children of broken families are especially likely to be "problem" children and a high concentration of such children is likely to increase juvenile delinquency. One manifestation has been the very adverse effect on schools in the neighborhood of a public housing project. Whereas a school can readily absorb a few "problem" children, it is very difficult for it to absorb a large number. Yet in some cases, broken families are a third or more of the total in a public housing project and the project may account for a majority of the children in the school. Had these families been assisted through cash grants, they would have been spread much more thinly through the community.

Minimum-wage laws

Minimum-wage laws are about as clear a case as one can find of a measure the effects of which are precisely the opposite of those intended by the men of goodwill who support it. Many proponents of minimum-wage laws quite properly deplore extremely low rates; they regard them as a sign of poverty; and they hope, by outlawing wage rates below some specified level, to reduce poverty. In fact, insofar as minimum-wage laws have any effect at all, their effect is clearly to increase poverty. The state can legislate a minimum wage rate. It can hardly require employers to hire at that minimum all who were formerly employed at wages below the minimum. It is clearly not in the interest of employers to do so. The effect of the minimum wage is therefore to make unemployment higher than it otherwise would be. Insofar as the low wage rates are in fact a sign of poverty, the people who are rendered unemployed are precisely those who can least afford to give up the income they had been receiving, small as it may appear to the people voting for the minimum wage.

This case is in one respect very much like public housing. In both, the people who are helped are visible—the people whose wages are raised; the people who occupy the publicly built units. The people who are hurt are anonymous and their problem is not clearly connected to its cause: the people who join the ranks of the unemployed or, more likely, are never employed in particular activities because of the existence of the minimum wage and are driven to even less remunerative activities or to the relief rolls; the people who are pressed ever closer together in the spreading slums that seem to be rather a sign of the need for more public housing than a consequence of the existing public housing.

A large part of the support for minimum-wage laws comes not from disinterested men of goodwill but from interested parties. For example, Northern trade unions and Northern firms threatened by Southern competition favor minimum-wage laws to reduce the competition from the South.

Farm price supports

Farm price supports are another example. Insofar as they can be justified at all on grounds other than the political fact that rural areas are overrepresented in the electoral college and Congress, it must be on the belief that farmers on the average have low incomes. Even if this be accepted as a fact, farm price supports do not accomplish the intended purpose of helping the farmers who need help. In the first place, benefits are, if anything, inverse to need, . . . [for] they are in proportion to the amount sold on the market. The impecunious farmer not only sells less on the market than the wealthier farmer; in addition, he gets a larger fraction of his income from products grown for his own use, and these do not qualify for the benefits. In the second place, the benefits, if any, to farmers from the price-support program are much smaller than the total amount spent. This is clearly true of the amount spent for storage and similar costs, which does not go to the farmer at all—indeed the suppliers of storage capacity and facilities may well be the major beneficiaries. It is equally true of the amount spent to purchase agricultural products. The farmer is thereby induced to spend additional sums on fertilizer, seed, machinery, and so on. At most, only the excess adds to his income. And finally, even this residual of a residual overstates the gain . . . [for] the effect of the program has been to keep more people on the farm than would otherwise have stayed there. Only the excess, if any, of what they can earn on the farm with the price-support program over what they can earn off the farm is a net benefit to them. The main effect of the purchase program has simply been to make farm output larger, not to raise the income per farmer.

Some of the costs of the farm purchase program are so obvious and well known as to need little more than mention: the consumer has paid twice, once in taxes for farm benefit payments, again by paying a higher price for food; the farmer has been saddled with onerous restrictions and detailed centralized control; the nation has been saddled with a spreading bureaucracy. There is, however, one set of costs which is less well-known. The farm program has been a major hindrance in the pursuit of foreign policy. In order to maintain a higher domestic than world price, it has been necessary to impose quotas on imports for many items. Erratic changes in our policy have had serious adverse effects on other countries. A high price for cotton encouraged other countries to enlarge their cotton production. When our high price led to an unwieldy stock of cotton, we proceeded to sell overseas at low prices and imposed heavy losses on the producers whom we had by our earlier actions encouraged to expand output. The list of similar cases could be multiplied. . . .

THE POOR IN THE WORK FORCE

Sar A. Levitan

Sar A. Levitan is a consultant to the W. E. Upjohn Institute for Employment Research, and is author of Federal Aid to Depressed Areas, *a recent comprehensive study of the ARA. In the following article Levitan focuses attention on several public programs—including unemployment insurance and the Neighborhood Youth Corps—which are concerned with the unemployed, and he considers the effectiveness of each in helping the poor. He explains that although the United States Employment Service and the unemployment-insurance program provide important services, the poorest people are not able to benefit greatly from them.*

UNEMPLOYMENT INSURANCE

Unemployment benefits have served as a base for essential income maintenance to those who are forced into idleness. However, the role of unemployment benefits as a substitute for wages in providing income maintenance should not be stretched. For example, in 1962 unemployment benefits offset only less than one fifth of the total loss in earnings of family heads. Available evidence would also suggest that unemployment insurance serves even to a lesser extent those whom we consider poor. About 15 million workers are not currently protected by unemployment insurance, including more than 6 million employed in agriculture, domestic service, and small firms with three or less workers, where many of the working poor tend to concentrate.

Aside from the restriction in coverage, it would appear that unemployment benefits have a limited applicability to the poor. In order to qualify for unemployment insurance, a worker has to earn a minimum of wages and/or be employed in a covered industry for a minimum of about

From "The Poor in the Work Force," by Sar A. Levitan, a paper prepared for the Chamber of Commerce of the United States, Task Force on Economic Growth and Opportunity. Reprinted by permission of Sar A. Levitan and the Chamber of Commerce of the United States.

fifteen weeks; the exact minimum earnings and duration of employment vary from state to state. Moreover, an unemployed worker qualified to receive unemployment benefits has to be available for work in order to collect benefits. The low wages which many of the working poor receive, and repeated spells of unemployment, may disqualify them from receiving benefits. In addition, . . . a large percentage of the idle poor are not available for work because of disability, illness, or home responsibilities.

The poor are also subject to prolonged spells of unemployment and even those of the unemployed poor who qualify for unemployment insurance frequently find that their benefits had exhausted before they gained new employment. Current proposals to extend unemployment benefits to thirty-nine weeks, instead of the . . . prevailing twenty-six weeks, would be of little aid to the poor. Proposals to extend [the] duration of benefits are normally restricted to unemployed persons who had considerable work experience in the past. For example, the Kennedy Administration proposed that extended benefits, financed by the federal government beyond twenty-six weeks' duration, would be limited to workers with at least seventy-eight weeks of employment during the preceding three years. Many of the poor—the exact number is unknown —do not have such work experience.

Whatever the merits of current proposals to raise unemployment benefits and extend their duration may be, they can hardly be justified on the basis that a liberalized program would aid the poor. This does not apply to the extension of coverage, particularly to domestic and agricultural workers. But for political and technical reasons, such extension of coverage is not likely to occur in the near future. The Kennedy Administration proposals to extend unemployment-insurance coverage did not include the above two groups.

The role of the unemployment-insurance program is to provide essential aid to the unemployed during periods of forced idleness. Reasonable people may disagree as to the proper level of the benefits and their duration. But it can hardly be argued that the role of unemployment benefits should be expanded to provide minimum income for the poor.

LABOR MARKET SERVICES

Existing public labor market operations are hardly geared to minister to the special needs of the poor and disadvantaged. The testing, counseling, and placement services of the public employment offices are oriented to the needs of employers who naturally tend to seek the best-qualified employees to fill existing job vacancies. And the public employment offices have devised techniques aimed at selecting [the] most-qualified applicants. The General Aptitude Test Battery (GATBY), given by the public employment service to the majority of applicants interviewed for placement, is designed to screen and test the literate.

It is, however, an established fact that the vast majority of the poor and disadvantaged unemployed have at best a limited education and many of them are illiterate. In 1963, the majority of all families whose head had less than eight years' education received an income below $3000. If the public employment service is to provide for the needs of the latter group, it will have to adopt new techniques to service the poorly educated. Of course, this does not mean that the employment service should neglect the needs of other unemployed workers, but to service the disadvantaged would require expanding the functions and activities of the employment services. . . . [Because] the public employment service is financed by federal funds, Congress and the Administration would have to recognize that the special services for the disadvantaged workers are usually costly and the resources allocated to the employment service would have to be increased. Otherwise, the performance of the special services to the disadvantaged will lead to the neglect of the employment service['s] regular functions.

The successful experience of vocational-rehabilitation programs provides ample justification for improving the quality of placement and related services for the disadvantaged workers.[1] The average expenditure is many times higher for each vocational-rehabilitation placement than for each employment-service placement. But such an investment is justified even on economic grounds.

The United States Employment Service does not publish any statistics relating to the educational attainment and other relevant characteristics of the employees serviced by the affiliated state employment offices. Such data are available about the trainees selected under the Manpower Development and Training Act [MDTA]. These statistics show that more than half of the MDTA trainees during fiscal 1964 had completed at least a high school education, while only a third of the unemployed in 1963 had attained a comparable educational level. On the other hand, only one of every twenty-one MDTA trainees had completed less than eight years of education, while one of every five unemployed was in that group.

In 1963, Congress recognized the special needs of the disadvantaged unemployed workers by providing training in basic education as part of a vocational course for those who lacked a rudimentary education, and the training period for them was extended to a maximum of seventy-two weeks, instead of the normal maximum of fifty-two weeks. However, the officials in charge of MDTA found it apparently difficult to implement the congressional intent and to develop adequate training techniques which would service the disadvantaged. A U.S. Department of Labor report recognized the difficulties of providing training for the illiterate, and acknowledged that the congressional intent "could not be implemented in time to be fully reflected in the fiscal year 1964 statistics." Whether MDTA training can be adapted to equip large numbers of the disadvantaged to fill existing job vacancies in the future remains debatable. . . .

YOUTH UNEMPLOYMENT

Youth unemployment has been a major problem in the United States during recent years. In 1964, youth unemployment averaged about 800,000, one of every seven in the labor force. Demographic factors alone would suggest that this problem might be accentuated in the immediate years ahead; a million more youths will reach age eighteen this year than during the past year. However, it would be a mistake to identify youth unemployment with poverty. The median family income of unemployed youths exceeded $6400 in 1964. But about 300,000 were members of families with an annual income of less than $5000 and half of these were in families with an annual income of less than $3000. An additional 150,000, in the same income brackets, were out of school and not in the labor force. Data are not available about the family size of these 450,000 teenagers. . . . [If we apply] the poverty criteria of the Social Security Administration, it might be estimated that about 400,000 of these youths were members of impoverished families.

The Economic Opportunity Act, the Great Society's version of the Poor Laws, places emphasis on providing work opportunities for impoverished idle youth. Over 40 per cent of the total funds authorized for the antipoverty program during the current fiscal year was allocated for youth programs. The CEA has estimated that the Neighborhood Youth Corps and the Job Corps will provide work and training opportunities for about 200,000 youths when these programs become fully operational later this year. MDTA will provide training opportunities for possibly another 25,000 youths. Existing programs should therefore absorb a significant proportion of impoverished unemployed and idle youth, if the above job expectations are materialized.

. . . [Because] the antipoverty program has barely started—the first youth camp was established . . . [early in 1964]—it is obviously premature to attempt any evaluation of this program. However, two basic issues may be raised at this point about the antipoverty youth programs.

The first issue deals with allocation of funds. It is estimated that the cost to the government per youth in the Job Corps will be three times as high as providing youth employment and training in the Neighborhood Youth Corps. The question has therefore been raised as to whether the limited funds available under the antipoverty program should not have been allocated to the Neighborhood Youth Corps in preference to the Job Corps program. Advocates of the current program argue that the rehabilitation of some youths from impoverished families will require uprooting them from their present unwholesome environment, which can be accomplished only in Youth Corps camps.

The second issue relates to the appropriate remuneration which should be paid to Neighborhood Youth Corps selectees. The decision has already been made that trainees will receive $1.25 per hour. This will mean that the youth attending school and selected for fifteen hours per week employment with the Neighborhood Youth Corps will receive almost as much as an MDTA youth trainee for forty hours of training (maximum MDTA allowance for youths is $20 per week). An out-of-school selectee for the Neighborhood Youth Corps will receive twice as much remuneration as the MDTA trainee. This policy will provide an overriding incentive for youths to compete for Neighborhood Youth Corps jobs, which normally will not lead to the acquisition of any particular skills, and forego more promising MDTA training. The situation will be even more aggravated in low-wage areas where the allowance under the Neighborhood Youth Corps will be considerably in excess of wages paid in private industry. This again will offer an incentive to youths to maintain Neighborhood Youth Corps jobs as long as possible, rather than seek private employment. A sound program would obviously dictate that the conditions be reversed. Moreover, . . . [because] it is expected that Neighborhood Youth Corps applicants will exceed the number of jobs that the program can provide under current funds, the question is raised whether it would not have been wiser to spread the limited funds available under the program to more youths.

1. Ronald Conley, *The Economics of Vocational Rehabilitation,* Chapter IV, unpublished doctoral dissertation, The Johns Hopkins University, 1964.

POVERTY AND UNEMPLOYMENT

Harry G. Johnson

Harry G. Johnson divides poverty into three types, but although he finds that somewhat different measures are required for each, he concludes that for all of them the most important thing the federal government can do is to adopt expansionary fiscal and monetary policies which will attack unemployment. Johnson is Professor of Economics at the University of Chicago. He is author of articles and books on a wide variety of theoretical and applied economic issues.

. . . Poverty in a basically free-enterprise economy like that of the United States can be conceived of as falling into three broad types: (1) poverty . . . [resulting from] failure of the economy to provide enough jobs for those able and willing to work, and capable of earning an adequate income if allowed to work; (2) poverty . . . [arising from] inability of individuals to contribute enough service to the productive process to earn an income above the poverty level; (3) poverty . . . [arising from] the existence of restrictions of greater or lesser severity on the opportunity for individuals to participate in the productive process to the full extent of their potential.

Poverty of the first type is ultimately the consequence of a failure of government policy to keep the level of demand for goods and services high enough to provide as many jobs as are wanted. This was a major cause of poverty in the 1930s, and has become a significant cause again since 1956. In the 1930s, the failure of policy was a consequence of governmental ignorance of how to manage the economy; recently, it has been a consequence, not of ignorance, but of consideration of other objectives of economic policy—first of the desire to prevent inflation, and then of the desire to improve the balance of payments. Poverty of this kind should, in my judgment, be handled by keeping aggregate demand at a

From "Poverty and Unemployment," by Harry G. Johnson. Reprinted by permission of Harry G. Johnson.

level adequate to provide the jobs required; if that is ruled out by other policy objectives, it seems to me incumbent on the economic managers to compensate the sufferers from unemployment by giving them decent unemployment benefits and, possibly, by [providing] training that will equip them for reabsorption in the labor force in ways that will not generate inflationary pressure or have adverse effects on the balance of payments. Poverty of the second type is essentially [the result of] immobility of the labor force, if immobility is conceived of broadly to include inability to acquire the skills necessary to earn a decent wage (either . . . [because of] innate deficiencies or deficiencies of family background), inability to move from contracting to expanding industries or occupations, and inability to move geographically. Poverty of this kind calls for government assistance to mobility, through the provision of educational facilities, employment services, and assistance for migration. At the same time it must be recognized that it may be cheaper to pay a poor person an adequate income than to try to train or retrain him or to relocate him. Our society has an aversion to eliminating poverty by the simple expedient of paying cash; but it is prepared to make an exception for the casualties of military service, and it seems to me that the casualties of economic progress deserve a similar consideration.

Poverty of the third type is essentially [the result of] discrimination; and it is more widespread than might appear at first sight. The notion that discrimination is responsible for the greater incidence of poverty among nonwhites is a familiar one, and has been thoroughly documented in recent years. But discrimination also underlies the plight of the aged poor, whom our society frequently forces to retire from remunerative work before their productive capacity and willingness to work are exhausted, and whom we are prepared to assist with public money only on condition that they do not work, or work only part-time for low wages. In a more subtle way, discrimination against the aged is involved in one of the important causes of aged poverty—the destruction of the real purchasing power of people's savings by inflation: in allowing unions and corporations to raise wages and prices, we sacrifice the economic interests of past participants in the productive process to those of present participants. Furthermore, discrimination is at the root of the high incidence of poverty among households headed by women, for our society discriminates against the participation of women in the labor force in countless ways—through giving women inferior education opportunities, through restricting the job opportunities open to them and denying them promotion, and through insisting that women with young children should remain home to look after them, which both prevents women from acquiring the employment experience necessary to enable them to command good jobs when they eventually have to support themselves, and prevents them from working if they find themselves in the position of heading families with young children. Finally, one suspects that discrimination is partly responsible for the association of poverty with low levels of educational attainment, in the sense that requirement of educational qualifications is often less . . . [that these are] essential for holding a particular job than . . . [that they serve] to narrow down the applicants that have to be considered to a manageable number.

As in the case of poverty . . . [caused by] immobility, there are two ways to tackle poverty . . . [arising from] discrimination. One is to direct policy at the elimination of discrimination; policies of this kind would involve preventing people who wish to discriminate against the nonwhite, the aged, the female, and the uneducated from doing so; bribing them not to do so by the expenditure of public funds; and investing in the development of the talents of the categories of humanity discriminated against. The other is to recognize that the exercise of discrimination is economically disadvantageous to those who are discriminated against, and to compensate them for it. Thus if we want older people to retire from the labor market—either because we want their jobs or because we think that work will be injurious to them—we should make it worth their while to retire, rather than push them out into poverty. Similarly, if we fear the competition of women, or think that society will gain more from the exercise of their child-rearing talents than from their economic activities, we should pay them enough to make them content with the role we assign them, instead of condemning them to poverty by preventing them from working. In elaborating on the second alternative, I have of course chosen the examples with respect to which there is a genuine problem of balancing considerations on both sides. There is no sense in bribing the nonwhite to remain economically inferior, or the uneducated to remain stupid; that is precisely why the proposal that they should be compensated for the disabilities imposed on them has been mentioned—to show the absurdity of these kinds of discrimination.

The foregoing analysis has drawn a sharp distinction between three sources of poverty: inadequate provision of jobs by governmental economic management, immobility of labor, and discrimination. This distinction, however, will not hold up in practice, because the second and third causes of poverty depend to a large extent on the first. When the aggregate demand for goods and services—and, therefore, for labor—is low, there will be little incentive for labor to move to higher-paying locations or occupations or higher grades of skill, and little incentive for employers to induce labor to undertake such movements. Similarly, when jobs are scarce, they will be rationed out to the already well-qualified worker, and denied to the talented but unskilled, to the nonwhite and the member of a religious minority, and to the female—whether single or married. Conversely, when jobs are plentiful and labor is hard to get, employers will have a strong incentive to increase the available supply of labor by investing in the upgrading of labor, by providing training for the unskilled and semiskilled, and by rearranging job responsibilities so that less skill is required for any particular component of a piece of work; they will also have an incentive to relax traditional practices discriminating against minority religions, nonwhites, and female employees. That this is so is amply borne out by wartime experience in the United States, when the pressure of strong demand for labor virtually destroyed anti-Semitism and introduced the most important victims of discrimination in the United States—Negroes and women—into a whole range of job opportunities to which they had previously been denied access. It is also exemplified by experience in the Soviet Union, where persistent labor shortage has resulted—among other things—in women constituting the majority of the medical profession and a substantial proportion of the engineering profession; in the United Kingdom, where a continuously low level of unemployment since the Second World War has fostered the easy absorption of a large number of immigrants from the less-developed countries of the British Commonwealth; and in the countries of the Common Market, where a tight labor market has fostered the absorption of vast numbers of immigrants from the less-developed countries of southern Europe.

The point is that most of the sources of poverty will gradually dissolve under the pressure of a high demand for labor. This point is extremely relevant to the problem of poverty in the United States, and to the whole [anti]poverty program. For it implies that the really effective solution to the problem of poverty lies in raising the level of demand for goods and services—and, therefore, for labor—to the point where poverty, instead of being part of the natural order of things, becomes a signal of economic waste that it will pay someone to take steps to eliminate. The key to the solution of the poverty problem, therefore, is not simply to try to educate and train the poor up to the point where someone will find them employable at a decent wage, but to raise demand so as to make labor scarce enough for it to be privately profitable to find a way of making the poor employable at a decent wage. Public policy, as embodied in the Economic Opportunity Act, can play a useful role in this solution, by helping to equip the poor to move up into a position among the nonpoor; and by so doing it can help to prevent a rise in aggregate demand from generating intolerable inflationary pressure. Public policy could also assist the process of reducing poverty by taking care of those who are too old or too inconveniently situated to make the upward move out of poverty, and to compensate those of the retired who are likely to be impoverished by the inflationary consequences of the shift to a tight market for labor. But in the absence of a policy of raising the demand for labor to the stretching point, ad hoc policies for remedying poverty by piecemeal assaults on particular poverty-associated characteristics are likely to prove both ineffective and expensive. The most effective way to attack poverty is to attack unemployment, not the symptoms of it. From this point of view, the most important thing the Administration did for the poor in 1964 was not to produce the Economic Opportunity Act, but to put through the tax cut, and to allow the rapid expansion of the money supply that has been permitted to occur despite fears of inflationary pressure.

LIBERTY AND EQUALITY

Gunnar Myrdal

Income transfers to the poor, "huge reforms" in education and training, and strengthening of trade unions are among the antipoverty measures that Gunnar Myrdal calls for. His emphasis on the "structural" character of unemployment in the United States contrasts with the view expressed in Professor Harry Johnson's article. Myrdal's comparison of the Social Security systems of the United States and his native Sweden is of particular interest. Gunnar Myrdal has been Swedish Minister of Commerce, and is now Professor of International Economics at Stockholm University. Among his other writings are An American Dilemma: The Negro Problem and Modern Democracy *and* Beyond the Welfare State.

ERADICATION OF POVERTY AS AN ECONOMIC INTEREST AND A NECESSITY FOR ECONOMIC PROGRESS

The moral issue has been touched upon as it is important, particularly so in the American nation which is basically moralistic and, at bottom, not very cynical. The "hard-boiled" social scientists in America, who are trying to forget that people have consciences and that this fact is of importance in the social and political processes, are wrong. More specifically they are reacting according to a common perversion of the nation's Puritanism.

. . . [Because] the eradication of poverty in America has now become an economic interest and almost a political necessity if America is to get out of the rut of relative economic stagnation with high and rising unemployment and underemployment, it is easy to forecast that moves for reform will come to be supported by strong moral sentiments. There is already a rising tide of moralism in the public debate on this issue as carried on in the literature and the press and by the political and intellectual leaders of the nation. The production of . . . comprehensive statistics . . . is itself an indication of the moral upsurge. Of the same nature is the flood of books on American poverty currently being written.

However, I now leave the moral issue and turn to the economics of the matter and to the policies that would turn the trend toward rapid and steady economic growth. In Chapter 2 [of my book] unemployment was first related to the discrepancy between the direction of labor demand and the quality of labor supply which gives the present unemployment its structural character. We found that, though the first condition for a reduction of unemployment must be a spurt to economic expansion, this will not take the country far toward full employment. Technological change will continue to release manual labor in agriculture and manufacturing industry, and the number of young workers entering the labor market without training for anything but manual labor will be increasing.

In order to reach full employment, public policy measures will have to be taken to raise the demand for such labor, mainly in construction work of various types. In order to enable the labor supply to meet this policy-induced increase and redirection of labor demand, large-scale training and retraining of workers will be needed. For the permanent achievement of full employment, huge reforms are needed in the field of education, including vocational training. These efforts will have to be directed primarily to the poverty-stricken sectors of the American society where unemployment and underemployment are concentrated and where the present opportunities are unsatisfactory.

These efforts have to be made and the expenditures paid for by public authority. The policy measures have to be planned for gradual realization. Under no circumstances can the goal be reached immediately. As high and rising unemployment is apt continually to worsen the preconditions for this type of policy, it is urgent that a start be made right away and on a large enough scale.

In Chapter 3 [of my book] we revealed the complex web through which a low level of education and training and, generally, low quality of labor supply is interrelated with poverty and all that poverty implies. The conclusion is that to be successful a full employment policy must aim at gradually eradicating poverty.

Efforts to educate and train the young and to re-educate those grown-ups who need it must meet with greater difficulties, be much less effective, and, consequently, even from a financial point of view imply more waste, the longer these people are poor, live in urban and rural slums, and are afflicted by all the other consequences of poverty. To an extent—but, as we know from experience, only to an extent——poverty will decrease as an effect of economic expansion and fuller employment. Direct measures of a surgical nature are needed at the same time. And they can be taken with less financial sacrifice on the part of the better-offs if the economy is progressing—indeed, so I am convinced, without any real sacrifice at all.

So far we have been discussing policies to change the supply of labor in order that it should better meet the demand for labor. However, an economic policy aimed at a reversal of the present trend of relative stagnation is even more fundamentally dependent upon an attack on poverty. The first condition for bringing down unemployment and for gradually reaching a full employment situation in America is certainly an expansion of production. Policy measures to induce an expansion of production imply an expansion of aggregate demand.

As a short-run proposition, an increase of aggregate demand can be achieved by a great variety of policies. Nothing is technically simpler than to start a boom. It could be done by spreading dollar notes as fertilizer from aeroplanes. From that point of view, and as the main thing is to get the economy going at full speed, it might seem that it should not be of great importance what particular policy measures are chosen.

But as the goal must be to reach not only a rapid but also a steady growth of the economy, it becomes important to be careful in choosing the policy means. The structural character of the present unemployment . . . makes it important that there be public investment in education, training, and retraining of workers right from the start. Otherwise scarcity of personnel with high levels of education and training will soon set a ceiling to the rise in production and most probably cause a recession long before anything in the neighborhood of full employment is achieved. As a low quality of part of the labor supply is intertwined with poverty in a vicious circle, there are reasons to take vigorous measures, also from the very start, to reduce poverty.

All this implies public expenditures which in the first place will improve the lot of the poor in America. The reason why such a redistributional economic policy will be of a general economic interest and not only benefit the poor themselves is, of course, that their unemployment and their low productivity when they are working is the main unutilized and underutilized resource in America. The majority of Americans now living in comfortable circumstances should, as a result of this policy, become better and not worse off than now. To get this dynamic thought understood and widely accepted is a major task for all efforts to public enlightenment in America.

The problem of economic expansion will . . . be dealt with in this chapter on the assumption that adequate measures are taken to prevent internal inflation and a deterioration of the country's international exchange position. . . .

REDISTRIBUTIONAL REFORMS

Redistributional reforms should be looked upon as equally important as a basis for the achievement of rapid and steady expansion of the American economy and high employment as from the point of view of social justice.

The reform that implies least government intervention in the economy is, of course, a reduction of the tax burden in the lower income brackets. The prevalence in the tax system of the United States—including the states and the municipalities—of taxes on real property and of sales taxes of various sorts implies, as a recent study by the Tax Foundation has revealed, that the tax burden in the lower and middle income strata is decisively regressive. This cannot possibly be in accordance with the nation's ideals for the distribution of the tax burden. A reform is overdue and would immediately put more purchasing power in the hands of those in America who are not consuming enough.

Nor would urgently needed reforms of the Social Security system require much government intervention in the economy. In this field the United States is still far behind the countries that share its basic values.

The treatment of old people in America, many of whom have a hard life behind them, is remarkable. Some basic facts illustrating the terrifying extent to which old people are left in poverty and destitution were given in the last chapter. They and their families, insofar as they have any, now represent one fourth of all poor people in America, a proportion that, if things are left as they are, will be increasing as their portion of the total population rises. It cannot possibly be the considered opinion of the majority of Americans that so many of those who in America are often called *senior citizens* should be left in misery, squalor, and often forbidding loneliness, unattended though they are in need of care. The situation is overripe for a radical reform of the old-age security system.

In Sweden all persons over sixty-seven will now, in stable currency, be guaranteed an income which, up to a fairly high level, shall amount to two thirds of what they earned in their best years. That the age limit could be placed so high is explained, first by the fact that there is a more accomplished system of Social Security for the sick, the invalid, and other needy groups. Moreover, in a full-employment economy, old people find a demand for their labor. As a matter of fact many over sixty-seven are also working. And more of them would be, if there was not an unfortunate tax rule discouraging them from having extra incomes; this tax rule will be changed in the continuous routine work on perfecting the details of the welfare state. The main problem left which is now eagerly discussed is how the economic security for the old can be supplemented by more of human care, so that old people should not be left so lonely in meeting their problems of life.

The United States is equally rich as Sweden. Most Americans believe they are much richer. They could certainly afford to be more generous to the old generation. In fact, I sincerely believe that the great majority of Americans, if they really were fully aware of the facts and saw the problem, should be eager to do it.

Likewise, it is impossible that the majority of good Americans really think that so many widows, divorced women, and unmarried mothers with their children should be left largely unaided. They also constitute one third of the poor in America.

The same must be true of the many families who are forced into poverty or destitution because the number of their children is so large. There are apparently no comprehensive statistics on the situation of families with numerous children. But from studies in other countries we know the crucial importance of this relationship. America is far behind most other rich countries in taking policy measures to prevent children from becoming a cause of poverty for their families and, at the same time, creating severe handicaps for their own advance in life.

Then we have the invalid and the sick. America can, of course, not long postpone creating a comprehensive system of pensions for invalids and of health insurance. It is possible, although difficult to imagine, that America may succeed in building up its health-insurance system to a greater part on the basis of voluntary insurance schemes than have other countries more advanced in this as in other fields of social welfare policy. But such a solution will then need to be supplemented by very substantial contributions from the government in order not to leave unaided so many of those who most need health protection and medical care, and who cannot afford to pay the premiums for private insurance.

The improvement of the unemployment-benefit system, particularly for the underemployed and the casually employed, belongs to the needed reforms of Social Security. It is not only a question of raising the level of unemployment benefits but of making them available on a national scale for all unemployed, even those having a shifting and menial job or not employed for a period long enough to qualify under present rules. The financial burden of an improvement of this form of Social Security —as of most others—will tend to be heaviest in the beginning, but to taper off as the economy expands and full employment is restored.

Related to Social Security reforms are a number of other reforms that do not require direct state intervention in the running of the economy. Thus it is urgently important that the minimum-wage legislation be made comprehensive and not as now inapplicable in many of the occupations where the setting of a wage floor is particularly important, as for instance in hotels and restaurants, some retail stores, hospitals, and laundries. Even after the change in the minimum legislation two years ago, some 16 million workers are not covered.

It is obvious that it is in the public interest that the mass of poor workers in these and in other low-paid jobs become organized in regular trade unions—and protected from exploitation by union racketeers. The task of organizing the majority of American workers who are outside the trade unions is, though not very forcefully, pursued by the American trade-union movement. The success of these efforts will be more assured, and the progress much more rapid, if the American economy is firmly set on the road to rapid and steady expansion.

The government itself, however, must take the responsibility of supplementing its agricultural policies in such a way that small farmers, small tenants, and farm workers are not left in poverty and destitution. In order not to make them permanent dole-takers, action will have to be taken to speed up the migration from rural slums, which again implies education, training, and retraining of the young and old workers settled there. Such policies also will have substantial results only when the economy is expanding rapidly and steadily.

OTHER GOVERNMENTAL ACTION

So far we have touched upon redistributive schemes that can be operated mainly on a cash basis or, in any case, without much government intervention in the economy. It should be clear, however, that in addition to those reforms there is a need for government policies that involve the government more directly in steering the economy, mostly by providing enterprise and services that properly belong to the public sector . . . [because] they cannot be expected to be forthcoming from private business. This, incidentally, is not a criticism of private business. Its proper role in the national economy of a democracy is to produce, sell, and make a profit as high as possible under the conditions created by the government, but not to create those conditions itself.

. . . [We] have already dealt with the urgent need of much greater efforts in the field of education and training of the young, particularly in the poorer strata, and of retraining old workers now afflicted by unemployment or employed in low-productivity occupations. We have also pointed out that this is not a simple matter, as teachers have to be educated and trained first. Implied is the need for a radical and comprehensive educational plan and an unemployment policy directed to [the] rehabilitation and reallocation of workers.

Almost the same is true in regard to health protection and medical care. The training of doctors and nurses must be considerably expanded and speeded up.

In filling these needs it will be necessary to allocate much larger resources to [the] building [of] schools and hospitals. In regard to the last item of badly needed increases of investment, it may be useful to compare the United States with Sweden, which is now far ahead of America both in regard to hospital beds per thousand inhabitants and the yearly increase of that important index. Even if President Kennedy's extremely limited proposal of medical aid to the aged were enacted— . . . [although] it does not meet the full need for hospital care for the chronically ill and does not pay for doctors and medicine—this would release a big demand that is now unsatisfied for hospital beds and also, of course, for doctors and nurses.

But there are many other public investments which are now irrationally neglected. There is, of course, no excuse for a rich country to tolerate huge slums in the big cities and lesser ones in the smaller cities, at the same time as it allows a large part of its manpower and other productive resources to go to waste. We have already pointed out that until now public efforts in the way of slum clearance have been feeble and mostly perverted in a way to favor the middle third of the nation but leave the poor in often worse slums than before. This has been the reality behind the euphemistic term *urban renewal*—which in Detroit is popularly referred to as *Negro removal*.

Closely related to the slum-clearance problem are all the other huge investments needed to make the American cities more effective as containers of human life and efficient work. These public investments become more urgently needed since now more than the total population increase goes to swell the number of city-dwellers and, in particular, the number of the inhabitants of the big metropolitan districts.

It is fairly generally recognized by those who have studied the problem, that there is a serious and irrational bias against public investment and consumption in America. It is a result of the combination of high-pressure salesmanship for private consumption and traditional suspicion against increasing public budgets. It cannot possibly correspond to what people would really prefer if they could as readily follow their impulses to buy the means of collective consumption as they can buy private consumers' goods, and if the former were equally well advertised.

SUGGESTED READINGS

Anderson, W. H. Locke. "Trickling Down: The Relationship Between Economic Growth and the Extent of Poverty Among American Families." *Quarterly Journal of Economics*, LXXVIII: 4 (November 1964), 511-24.

Bowman, Mary Jean, and W. Warren Haynes. *Resources and People in East Kentucky; Problems and Potentials of a Lagging Economy.* Baltimore: The Johns Hopkins University Press, 1963.

Caplovitz, David. *The Poor Pay More: Consumer Practices of Low-Income Families.* New York: The Free Press of Glencoe, Inc., 1963.

Cater, Douglas. "The Politics of Poverty." *The Reporter*, XXX (February 13, 1964), 16-20.

Caudill, Harry. *Night Comes to the Cumberlands: A Biography of a Depressed Area.* Boston, Atlantic-Little, Brown, 1963.

Conant, James B. *Slums and the Suburbs.* New York: McGraw-Hill Book Company, Inc., 1961.

Epstein, Lenore A. "Unmet Need in a Land of Abundance," *Social Security Bulletin* XXVI (May 1963), 3-11.

Faltermayer, Edmund K. "Who Are the American Poor?" *Fortune*, LXVI (March 1964), 118-19, 218-24, 229.

Galbraith, John Kenneth. "Let Us Begin: An Invitation to Action on Poverty." *Harper's Magazine*, CCVIII (March 1964), 16, 18, 23, 24, 26.

Galloway, L. E. "The Foundations of the 'War on Poverty.' " *American Economic Review*, LV: 1 (March 1965), 122-30.

Jencks, Christopher. "Johnson vs. Poverty." *The New Republic*, CL (March 28, 1964), 15-18.

Johnson, Haynes. "Poverty in Appalachia." *Washington Star.* Eleven-part series (February 9-14, 16-20, 1964).

Lampman, Robert J. "Approaches to the Reduction of Poverty," *American Economic Review: Papers and Proceedings*, LV (May 1965), 521-29.

MacDonald, Dwight. "Our Invisible Poor." *The New Yorker*, XXXVIII (January 19, 1963), 82, 84, 86, 88, 91-92.

May, Edgar. *The Wasted Americans.* New York: Harper & Row, Publishers, 1964.

Miller, Herman P. "Is the Income Gap Closing?" *The New York Times Magazine* (November 11, 1963), 50-58.

Miller, Herman P. *Rich Man, Poor Man.* New York: Thomas Y. Crowell Company, 1964.

Morgan, James N., *et al.*, *Income and Welfare in the United States.* New York: McGraw-Hill Book Company, Inc., 1962.

Myrdal, Gunnar. "The War on Poverty." *New Republic,* CL (February 8, 1964), 14-17.

Orshansky, Mollie. "Who's Who Among the Poor: A Demographic View." *Social Security Bulletin* XXVIII (July 1965), 3-32.

Perkins, Ellen J. "Unmet Need in Public Assistance," *Social Security Bulletin,* XXIII (April 1960), 3-11.

Pond, M. Allen. "Interrelationships of Poverty and Disease," *Public Health Reports,* LXXVI (November 1961), 967-73.

"Poverty in America," *The New Leader,* XLVII (March 30, 1964).

"Poverty U.S.A." *Newsweek,* LXIII (February 17, 1963), 19-20, 23-38.

"The Question of a Separate Federal Program for the Development of 'Appalachia,' Pro and Con." *Congressional Digest,* XLIX (December 1964), 289-314.

Schorr, Alvin L. *Slums and Social Insecurity.* Research Report No. 1, Social Security Administration. Washington, D.C.: USGPO, 1963.

Schultz, Theodore W. "Investing in Poor People: An Economist's View." *American Economic Review: Papers and Proceedings,* LV (May 1965), 510-20.

Task Force on Economic Growth and Opportunity, *The Concept of Poverty.* Washington, D.C.: Chamber of Commerce of the United States, 1965.

Theobald, Robert. "Poverty in the Affluent Society." *Challenge,* XI (January 1963), 22-24.

"The Vicious Cycle of Poverty." *Business Week,* 1796 (February 1, 1964), 38-43.

"Waging War on Poverty." *The American Federationist,* LXXI (April 1964), 1-8.

Walinsky, Adam. "Keeping the Poor in Their Place: Notes on the Importance of Being One-Up." *The New Republic,* CLI (July 4, 1964), 15-18.